D0803983

a String of Pearls

Also by Bettie B. Youngs, Ph.D.

Taste Berries for Teens: Inspirational Stories and Encouragement on Life, Love, Friendship and Tough Issues (Health Communications, Inc.)

Taste-Berry Tales: Stories to Lift the Spirit, Fill the Heart and Feed the Soul (Health Communications, Inc.)

Gifts of the Heart: Stories That Celebrate Life's Defining Moments (Health Communications, Inc.)

Values from the Heartland: Inspirational Stories of Values in Action (Health Communications, Inc.)

Getting Back Together: How to Create a New Loving Relationship with Your Old Partner and Make It Last! (Adams Media Corp.)

Is Your Net-Working? A Complete Guide to Building Contacts and Career Visibility (John Wiley)

Stress & Your Child: Helping Kids Cope with the Strains & Pressures of Life (Random House)

Safeguarding Your Teenager from the Dragons of Life: A Guide to the Adolescent Years (Health Communications, Inc.)

How to Develop Self-Esteem in Your Child: 6 Vital Ingredients (Macmillan/Ballantine)

Self-Esteem for Educators: It's Job Criteria #1 (Jalmar Press)

Keeping Our Children Safe: A Guide to Emotional, Physical, Intellectual and Spiritual Wellness (John Knox/Westminster Press)

You and Self-Esteem: A Book for Young People (Jalmar Press)

Managing Your Response to Stress: A Guide for Administrators (Jalmar Press)

a String of Pearls

Bettie B. Youngs, Ph.D.

Adams Media Corporation
Holbrook, Massachusetts

Copyright ©2000, Bettie B. Youngs.
All rights reserved. This book, or parts thereof, may not be reproduced
in any form without permission from the publisher; exceptions are made
for brief excerpts used in published reviews.

Published by
Adams Media Corporation
260 Center Street, Holbrook, MA 02343. U.S.A.

ISBN: 1-58062-278-X

Printed in Canada.

J I H G F E D C B A

Library of Congress Cataloging-in-Publication Data
Youngs, Bettie B.
String of pearls : inspirational stories celebrating the resiliency
of the human spirit / Bettie B. Youngs.
p.   cm.
ISBN 1-58062-278-X
1. Suffering. 2. Conduct of life. I. Title.
BJ1409 . Y68   2000
170'.44--dc21   00-020324
CIP

"Footprints" by Margaret Fishback Powers, ©1964 Margaret Fishback Powers, Grand
Rapids, MI: Zondervan Publishing House. Reprinted with permission.

"Cliffs Notes on the Heart" by Bettie B. Youngs, Ph.D. from *Gifts of the Heart*,
©Bettie B. Youngs, Ph.D. Deerfield Beach, Florida: HCI, 1998. Reprinted with permission.

This publication is designed to provide accurate and authoritative information with regard to
the subject matter covered. It is sold with the understanding that the publisher is not engaged
in rendering legal, accounting, or other professional advice. If legal advice or other expert
assistance is required, the services of a competent professional person should be sought.
—From a *Declaration of Principles* jointly adopted
by a Committee of the American Bar Association and a Committee
of Publishers and Associations

Artwork on page 138 by Mark Rimland, printed with permission.

This book is available at quantity discounts for bulk purchases.
For information, call 1-800-872-5627.

Visit our exciting Web site at www.adamsmedia.com

"God whispers to us in our pleasures, speaks in our conscience, but shouts in our pains; it is His megaphone to rouse a deaf world."
—C.S. Lewis

This book is lovingly dedicated to my nephew, Aaron Burres. You have taught us all a little more respect for the days we are given, shown us the meaning of courage and allowed us to glimpse the depth of our love for you.

Table of Contents

~ Contents ~

Acknowledgments

This book, for me, has been an exercise in gaining a truer appreciation for the nature and inner workings of the human spirit. Although there are only some 31 stories profiled in this book, I listened to literally hundreds upon hundreds of courageous people share how a trying time granted greater meaning to the significance and purpose of their lives. As they began to understand the lesson that unfolded in the wake of heartache, they evaluated themselves and their lives, often coming to the conclusion they wanted to live *more* fully.

There were other insights, too. In ordinary times we use but a fraction of our potential. But when things are tough, we draw upon an amazing reserve and find ourselves extraordinarily more resilient than imagined. Perseverance is a rebirth of sorts. This was evident time and time again for those who confronted an obstacle and made their way to the other side. I experienced this firsthand just as I was completing this book. My brother's seventeen-year-old son was hit in a high-speed accident while driving to homecoming festivities. For the next fifteen days following the accident, he lay in a coma. As he did, his stunned parents found within themselves a heroic energy, one that demanded and supported among other things, their around-the-clock caretaking for their son: talking to him, reading to him, singing to him, praying for him. Nonstop. Not a moment went by without his being surrounded and supported by their love. Their son emerged from the coma, and now other challenges await. Like old pros, his parents now confront these new challenges with a different *knowing*. A different sort of peace, but with the same heroic energy.

We humans are amazing. Durable. Resilient. Love-giving. Love-needing.

I would like to thank the many people who so generously shared their life-changing and life-affirming experiences in the writing of this book. May we *hear* their stories to more fully appreciate our own. Though there are too many names to list individually, I honor each of you so much; you are near and dear to my heart.

To my publisher, Bob Adams, and the wonderful staff at Adams Media—a very special thanks! Bob has been wanting me to do this book for years, and I am happy to once again work with him. His vision in publishing raises the bar for the quality of inner life so it's an honor for me to grow worthy of these goals in my work. To the editorial staff, Ed Walters, Dawn Thompson, and especially Paula Munier Lee—your encouragement, support, and professional assistance is just the *best!* And a special thanks to my staff and, in particular, Tina Moreno and Jennifer Leigh Youngs. This book was an enormous undertaking and your talent was invaluable.

Deepest appreciation and love to my mother, Arlene Burres, who taught me that to write is to experience life in many forms. This glorious woman is a pillar of strength to me and to every member of her family. As always, to my father, Everett, who continues to teach me the boundlessness of courage and real strength. His staunch friendship is welded into my heart and, as such, is a constant source of support and joy. To Jennifer Leigh Youngs, my daughter, who holds the strings—and the pink slip—to my heart. Because of her I've learned to love more deeply than I ever could have imagined, and she's been the inspiration for a few tribulations as well! To my husband, David Kirk, for his genuine love and joy and friendship. And as always, glory to God from whom all blessings flow.

Introduction

This is a book of inspiration, accounts that show the phenomenal resiliency and boundless majesty of the human spirit. Through the people we meet within these pages, we learn that we *can* endure a great deal, and that we can triumph over adversity. Their stories teach us that tribulation is fuel in the soul's journey to become wiser, more astute, compassionate, and loving, and that the heart actually *uses* tough times to show us our potential as humans. While happiness feeds the heart, it is tribulation that *opens* the soul.

What a gracious outcome, what a miraculous knowing. At the depth of our heartache lies the height and strength of our nobility as human beings.

In the same manner in which a pearl evolves from an invading grain of sand, the intrusion of disappointment and heartache can be transformed into a thing of beauty and value in our lives. Provocation and sorrow are important messengers on life, love, and truth. Difficult times, obstacles, and heartbreak are cataclysmic experiences that ask us to focus, to question not only *what* we are doing but *why,* granting us the opportunity to come to terms with our lives in an honest way. Making peace with our inner truths can move us closer to discovering the real meaning and purpose of our lives, to make the shift away from simply "living life," to instead, living fully within our own lives. It's not just the mountain we conquer, but ourselves.

To that end, trial and tribulation serve to alert us, mold us, direct us, and unite us.

To alert us: As much as we may want to avoid the calamities of life, they serve a purpose. Heartache is merely a symptom, a siren or bell that sounds when the soul is in need of our personal attention.

To mold us: The hardships of life shape us to be more mature in our faith, more compassionate to ourselves, and more understanding of others.

To direct us: Times of trial can force us to look beyond our immediate circumstances, to ask questions such as, "What is the purpose of my life?" This introspection leads us to rethink priorities, goals, and values, so that we are able to see our lives more clearly and can move closer to God, to ourselves, and to others.

To unite us: Reminding us how fragile we really are, our struggles show us how much we need each other. In reaching out, we draw closer and are strengthened by this unity, as the very nature of *sharing* our burdens lightens our load.

Tribulation and heartache are not selective in whom they call upon. Inevitably, each of us will face times of sadness, sorrow, or challenge in our lives—whether in the form of physical pain, emotional anguish, heartbreak, disappointment, humiliation, loss, grief, or challenge.

There is no hierarchy to the things that trouble us. We cannot measure one loss against another loss, nor one pain against another pain. We must celebrate the ultimate harvest of the pearl—and not dwell on the source of our pain. It is then that we are able to yield the praiseworthy attributes on the other side.

Each of the stories in this book illuminates how suffering can be transformed into a priceless jewel: renewed courage, hope, endurance, wisdom, faith, or love. Each is a testimony to the majesty of the heart and soul to win the fight for light over shadow.

May these stories grant us the wisdom to more fully appreciate our own resilience, impart the courage to endure trial and tribulation, and serve as a pearl of light for all of us as we walk through our own dark nights.

Exactly Right

"Destiny grants our wishes, but in its own way, in order to give us something beyond our wishes."

—GOETHE

Johnny! Johnny! Johnny!" the fans cheered, their exuberant voices rising above the stomping feet, whistles, claps, and the rumbling and thundering of the shaking stadium. It was New Year's Day, 1993, and their team, the University of Alabama, had just won the National Football Championship. Johnny, flanked by his parents, the players, and an assortment of fans—and ebullient to the point of cheering on his own behalf—offered high-fives to every available hand. He loved this game and everything and everyone associated with it!

Even though a veteran to football crowds, and considered a hero in the locker room and on the field, not once did Johnny take the fans' pleas for autographs lightly. Caught up in the crowd's joyous fervor, the exalted member of the team with the bright, shining eyes shouted, "We're number one! We're number one! We're number one!" and happily signed as many autographs as possible. Tonight, once again, Johnny was a hero.

Many say Johnny Stallings has been a hero from day one.

Well, maybe not from day *one*.

When Johnny was born, his father, Gene Stallings, was nothing short of ecstatic. A former football star and already a respected and renowned football coach, Gene and his wife Ruth Ann already had two daughters. Gene absolutely adored his little girls, but girls couldn't follow in his footsteps in the powerful and exciting world of football. But a son could. And a son could carry on the family name: Eugene Clifton Stallings, III, after Gene and his father. And now Gene had a son! All the plans and expectations, all those dreams that someday *when he had a son* would come true. On a winner of a day in June of 1962 — the 11th, to be exact — baby boy Stallings was born.

As the new father of a future football player with Heisman Trophy potential walked out the double doors of the hospital that day, he could see it all now: The ball had been thrown to his handsome and burly son, who leaped up and coolly plucked the pass from the air. Gene could just hear the rambunctious crowd of loyal fans cheer at yet another remarkable performance of this majestic athlete. Then, Eugene Clifton Stallings, III, tucked the ball under his arm, and with long agile strides, made his way towards the goal line. Oh, yes. Gene's happiness was full. His boy would make him so proud. Heading towards his car, his face literally beaming, he envisioned his strapping son going the distance for the touchdown, spiking the ball victoriously to the ground. The band struck up a note, the cheerleaders did their victory dance, and the crowd exploded into an uproar of joyous hoots, hollers, and wild applause! Yes, he'd start working with his son as soon as the boy was ready.

Gene himself had started playing football while only in the fourth grade and was captain of his football team in high school. Four years later, right on schedule, he was captain of his college team—a team coached by his future boss and mentor, Bear Bryant. Everything centered on football. Gene even postponed marrying Ruth Ann, his high school sweetheart, until he completed his final game as a college senior! And now Gene had a son who could carry on the tradition of playing football—maybe even play on a team he coached. Again, a clear vision came to Gene. This time it was a Super Bowl game and he was coaching it. Of course, his son was starting quarterback! There he was, a brawny youth, intercepting a pass, skillfully curling the football under his arm and racing down the field for a heroic touchdown. Gene started his car, aglow with dreams. Life was good. As a matter of fact, life was just perfect.

But just hours later, when Gene returned to the hospital, his dreams were shattered. Gene learned his newborn son wasn't destined to play football *at all*. "Your son has Down syndrome," the doctors informed him.

At first, Gene refused to believe them. When their baby boy was brought to him and Ruth Ann in the hospital, Gene slowly looked over the infant cradled in his arms. He carefully surveyed the baby's soft, smooth skin, ran his fingers across his bald little head and touched each of his ten tiny fingers and toes, then his button nose—like he had when he held his daughters for the first time. The little boy looked okay to him. To Gene's eye, he looked much like their baby daughters had at birth. Surely the doctors were wrong. Surely the baby's sleepiness and sallow skin could well be attributed to the fact that he was born prematurely—a whole month early.

But the doctors were right about baby boy Stallings. Chromosome tests confirmed conclusively that their son had Down syndrome. It was official. Gene Stallings's son would never be "normal"—let alone play football. And so, because he wouldn't be able to pass on the family name—nor carry on Gene's legacy—the name "Eugene Clifton Stallings, III" would be held in reserve for a "perfect" son. Instead, the little boy in Gene's arms was given the biblical name John Mark.

The doctors and some of their friends urged the Stallingses to put Johnny in an institution for children with severe disabilities. "It will make life easier on the family," they said. One friend warned, "The baby will become such a burden to the girls." Another predicted, "A retarded child will hinder your chances of continuing as a successful coach." Johnny's doctor said he didn't think Gene and Ruth Ann were up to the demands of raising "this kind of child." But sending their son to an institution didn't feel right to the little boy's parents. Johnny was theirs to love and raise—no matter how he might look . . . no matter how he would act. They vowed to provide the love and special care their son needed to develop in all the ways he could.

How Johnny "looked and acted" did take some adjustments. Their friends didn't quite know what to say about the Stallingses' "retarded" child. They especially didn't know what to say to Gene. They knew how excited he was to have a son and pretty much knew that a son of Coach Gene Stallings would be encouraged and guided to embrace sports—namely, football. At work, people's voices lowered when the subject of Johnny came up, and friends and colleagues were uneasy when they came to the Stallingses' home.

Though he tried to be cheerful and optimistic, perhaps no one was more disappointed than Gene himself, who felt a tremendous sense of loss over the dreams—now dashed—he once held for this son.

At first work provided an escape. Being swamped with activities distracted him from his mind's ever-present concerns over the responsibilities of raising a child with special needs. But gradually his sense of burden was transformed by the peace, love, and calm that enveloped him when he held his son. He sensed Johnny needed him. And soon, he knew he needed Johnny—a gentle, loving child who provided a space for tranquility in an otherwise tough and competitive world, and an all too hectic life.

But love couldn't cure the baby's mounting physical problems. Johnny had trouble breathing and his stomach grew distended. The Stallingses learned their son had a life-threatening defect called Eisenmenger syndrome—a hole between the chambers of the heart that severely hinders the body from getting the oxygen it needs. Now even childhood illnesses held the threat of possibly being fatal. Gene had trouble accepting that his son was so fragile. All day long he was surrounded by football players who had been blessed with strong bodies and were naturally athletic and then came home to frail Johnny. He yearned for his son to have just a fraction of their ability and strength.

But Johnny did possess ability and strengths. They were just different from those Gene admired in his athletes on the field. The first glimmer came when, one evening after an arduous day of work, his daughters rushed out to greet him. "Come on, Daddy, come on," the girls squealed, tugging Gene around to the back of the house. Standing on the patio, holding onto the dog, Johnny spotted Gene and smiled. Suddenly, the little boy let go of the dog and tottered across the patio. When he got to the other end, Johnny turned to look at Gene and laughed, clapping his hands. Glowing with satisfaction and joy, Johnny knew he had accomplished quite a feat and was very proud of himself for it! Scooping his son into his arms and laughing with him, Gene saw that Johnny could be capable. The girls, who had worked diligently each day with Johnny, had found a way to help him walk — even though doctors said he never would.

One Sunday while the Stallings family was at church, Gene cuddled Johnny on his lap. As he bent his head to pray, he noticed a dark red stain spreading on his slacks. Lifting Johnny up, Gene gasped. The child's outfit was soaked with blood. Johnny was rushed to the hospital, where he was immediately prepped for surgery. He had an ulcer in his intestine and was bleeding internally. Ruth Ann and Gene realized the extent of the problem: surgery was necessary and yet, their son might die because of it. Doctors had warned that Johnny should never be given anesthesia because his circulatory system couldn't carry enough oxygen while he was sedated. "You need to handle this *exactly* right," Gene pleaded. "You give him enough anesthesia, but not a drop too much. It has to be *exactly* right. *Exactly*."

The amount turned out to be "exactly right," and not just because Gene had ordered it. Gene knew that his son had a special effect on people. On this day, the anesthesiologist was added to the list of those who genuinely liked and intuitively admired this very special little boy. As Gene and Ruth Ann slept on cots in their son's room on the night of Johnny's surgery, Gene saw the anesthesiologist slip into the room and take a seat in the straight-back chair beside Johnny's bed. As he dozed fitfully all night, Gene kept vigil. Always the doctor was there, stroking Johnny's forehead with the back of his hand and making certain the I.V. line stayed untangled. He didn't leave the room until the first rays of daylight streaked through the blinds. Gene was touched by the man's care of his son — and knew that Johnny had inspired it. It was becoming more apparent to Gene that Johnny's life was like a beacon of hope, symbolic of determination. If this little boy could courageously confront the obstacles in his life and be so cheerful, then they could, too.

Johnny's brush with death had given Gene a new kind of intensity and vitality. On a particularly bleak Friday, Coach Stallings gathered his players in the locker room. The season wasn't going well; they had only won one of six games they'd played. A "pep talk" was in order. For the first time, Gene talked openly about Johnny and what he'd gone through in his young life. "Johnny is such a fighter. He's made it against the odds, and you can, too," Gene reassured his players. Silence filled the locker room as the coach spoke. This was a real story of inspiration, a story the players could rally behind. It made them admire their coach even more than they already did. A committed and determined team took to the field in a way they'd never seized it before.

They won that game. And the next. And the next, and the next.

When Johnny was ten, Gene took the job of coach for the Dallas Cowboys. More entrenched in his work than ever, he had less time to spend with his family, but was determined to find a way to change that. He carefully considered the possibility of taking Johnny to football practice with him — weighing the benefits of the time they could spend together against the possible risks of Johnny's being hurt by the comments and remarks of others.

Gene needn't have worried about how his son would be received. Johnny's winning personality instantly gained the respect and acceptance of the players. Gene watched as Johnny looked up at the players, men four times his size, making eye contact, greeting each one by name, then shaking their hands. Responding to his bright disposition and gentle nature, his humor, his kindness, and his courage, it was easy to see the players genuinely liked him. Many of the players brought their own children with them to the weekend practice sessions. And they were touched by Johnny's generosity, which was especially evident when he played with their children. Invariably one of the players would give Johnny a football, and invariably, by the time practice was over, Johnny had given it to another child. While this spirit of giving surprised the players, it didn't surprise Gene. Thinking of others was one of Johnny's many admirable traits. Another was Johnny's ability to never forget a name or face once he met someone. If Gene forgot a player's name—or nickname—Johnny would unfailingly provide his father with the player's name! When it was time to leave after each practice, Gene would watch his frail son hug each of these huge men—a sight that always filled his heart with tenderness, gratitude, and admiration.

Gene went on to coach other teams, and Johnny was there, standing on the sidelines next to his father. It became not only something very special between father and son, but a legacy the world would never forget. Certainly it was important to the teams Gene Stallings coached. Standing at his father's side, Johnny's presence brought something special to every team, the simple message to "do the best you can with what you've got." And so, Johnny on the field alongside his father was not only a common sight, but a necessary one. The relationship between their coach and his son somehow lifted up the spirit of the whole team, and the fans as well. Just the sight of father and son—Gene and Johnny—was an inspiration that took on a personality of its own.

In 1996, seven years after returning to the University of Alabama to take the job of head coach, Gene decided it was time to retire in order to spend more time with Johnny. He could see his son was slowing down (his health still remained fragile). He wanted time to ride horses with Johnny and to fish and do chores alongside his son on their cattle ranch. Today they amble on horseback across the ranch.

Seeing them together, their mutual love and admiration apparent, is a vision that opens our hearts to acknowledge that though we are all different, we are needed by each other. "Johnny is such a blessing to me," says the coach. "And an inspiration. More than anyone else, it is Johnny who taught me about courage, about empathy—and, most of all, about total, unconditional love. I've enjoyed my wins, but none can compare to the joy I get by spending time with Johnny. He's taught the players on my teams how to commit with all their might, how to really be there for someone. He, more than anyone I've ever known, knows how to play the game of life. He does it so well. He does it exactly right. I remember the day I was told he had Down syndrome, wondering how my world had suddenly gone wrong. But in fact, on that day everything in my life was going 'exactly right.'"

Johnny may not have been the football hero his father once envisioned, but caring for his son offered Gene a pearl of even greater prize and perspective than the one he had imagined and sought. Thankfully, *exactly right* is not left to us to choose, but rather, a decision of spirit, one that knows no mediocrity of soul: It recognizes the gentle, fragile, and frail, as much as the mighty, strong, and robust, as needed members of the same team—the human race.

When we accept the tidings life brings, we learn that even when hopes and dreams don't unfold exactly as planned, they may be even better—they may be *exactly right*.

Fairy-Tale Rescue

"Each friend represents a world in us, a world possibly not born until they arrive."

—ANAÏS NIN

"Take me home," the ad read. "My family had to move on without me and now I'm all alone. But they didn't leave me because I'm unlovable. I'm very adorable as you can see." The photo above the ad showed a gold-colored dog with his large ears drooping forlornly, his dark eyes mournful and beseeching. "I'm friendly and loyal," the ad went on to promise, "not to mention smart. Can we strike up a partnership?" it coaxed. "Let's shake on it!" There the dog sat, his paw held up to "shake." Philip Gonzalez smiled to himself. Picking up the ads called *The Paw Print Press*, he started to read them out of sheer boredom. But now he wondered . . . a pet? Maybe he needed a pet.

Having been a steamfitter, recently Philip was permanently disabled when his arm was badly injured on the job.
Unable to work, his life had suddenly taken a hard turn. The
boredom was bad enough, but on top of that he felt so hopeless—the lonely hours stretching before him, day in and day
out, with nothing of any use to do. He continued reading the
Humane Society ads, the idea of owning a pet slowly taking
hold. Beside the photo—a black and white English Cocker
Spaniel—he read, "I'm very calm and I'm the perfect lap
dog. My name is Nigel and I'm an eight-year-old male. I'm
housebroken and would love to share your couch with you.
Please come spend some time with me." Philip looked at the
photo again, the dog's imploring eyes seemed to beg for a
visit. Next he read about a Sheltie named Shoelaces who
reported that he had been "abandoned and abused. . . . "
Philip twinged at the plight of the pooch. "I need an especially compassionate someone to love and care for me." The
words tugged at Philip's heavy heart. Maybe caring for a dog
might be just what he needed; certainly he could use a companion who needed him.

As he studied the page in his hands, Philip's eyes traveled
next to a cat named Tawny who was also looking for a home.
"As an adult female cat, I enjoy other cats! I have delicate,
almond shaped eyes," she cajoled in a shameless attempt to sell
herself. Hmmm, a cat? Maybe he would like to have a cat.
He'd always liked cats. Philip looked at the picture of another
one, Ernestina, who promised she was "not only big in size,
but also big in personality." Then he scrutinized Sasha, a
feline with long black hair, who asked, "Is there room in your
heart and home for me?"

Finding himself wishing he could take them all in, Philip
returned to looking at the dogs again. "You'll find me a comforting companion," the caption under yet another dog read. "I

no longer fit into my family's schedule. They traveled a lot and I was often left to fend for myself. But that was the least of my worries. What I miss most are the gentle hands of their son who went away to college, and the gaiety and laughter of his voice, the jogs through the neighborhood, the feel of love in action." Philip longed for "love in action," too. The dog in the picture looked a little on the skinny side, as though he needed some TLC. Philip concluded that at this point in his life, he had nothing but time on his hands and so could give a doggie some tender loving care. Besides, anything that might lift the oppressive weight of feeling so inadequate was worth a try.

He decided to pay a visit to the Humane Society.

Philip Gonzalez walked into the animal shelter, a man on a mission. Unable to shake off the depression that had been haunting him for months now, the classified ads had provided a possible remedy. His self-prescribed cure was to adopt an animal who had it harder than him, one who would appreciate his care and companionship—a dog to take care of and to love. Taking out the ads, he flipped to the dog he had circled and marked #1. "This is the right one," he announced to the animal control officer, "or else this one," he said, pointing at the dog he had marked #2. He was disappointed to learn that both dogs had already been adopted, but he was immediately assured there were many others to choose from—all in equally as great a need of love and care. As he strolled slowly from one pen of barking dogs to the next, Philip stopped at each one to study every canine, hopeful he would know when he saw a new "right one." He paused at the enclosure of a dog who was not barking.

Ginny, a Siberian husky–schnauzer mix, lay feeling desolate in a corner of the pen she shared with four other dogs. She, too, had fallen on some hard times. She and her three puppies had been found starving in an abandoned apartment. Now, she lay on concrete, behind bars, with a maternal heart that ached for her puppies. Cute and playful, they'd all been adopted quickly, leaving the young mother all alone and feeling deserted. Like Philip, she didn't know what lay ahead for her, and so pined not only over her loss but also the uncertainties of her future.

When the brown-haired man wearing jeans and a T-shirt stopped in front of her pen, Ginny peered listlessly up at him. She watched the smile starting to pull beneath his mustache, then glanced back to his kind eyes. They were large, round, dark eyes—friendly, but a little sad, too. Roused by something about the man, Ginny stood up and trotted slowly to the fence to get a friendlier look at him.

Philip stared at the tan dog with large dark eyes set off by furry white eyebrows. She had the same white fur around her nose, mouth, cheeks, and chest. Her tan ears stuck straight up, trimmed in black. She was no pedigree or purebred, no frisky puppy, and so far as classic definitions went, she was not much in the looks department. But something soulful about her resigned gaze struck a benevolent chord in Philip. He was drawn to her and stood silently, as though assessing her. As though she sensed his growing affection, Ginny's tail thumped slowly to life. And when he stooped down and reached his fingers through the fence to touch her tenderly, the doggie's tail picked up speed. She barked a single syllable—which Philip interpreted as an omen of greeting to a kindred soul—then she pawed at the wire that separated them. Philip laughed and promised, "Okay, you're the one." Then, borrowing a line from the movie *Pretty Woman*, he asked the dog, "So, if I rescue you, will you rescue me?" In that cinematic love story, Richard Gere plays a rich, successful businessman, who asks Julia Roberts, a woman of the streets who he has unwillingly fallen in love with, what it is that she wants. "The whole fairy tale," Julia answers. "So if I rescue you," he asks, "then what?" She replies with sincerity, "I'll rescue you, right back," implying that they both need each other. It was the same deal struck between man and dog that day. And it's exactly what Philip and Ginny have done for each other since. Both in need of love and companionship, they rescued each other from the heartache of braving hard times all alone.

But being rescued and being needed isn't all each has done for the other. Ginny took "rescue" to heart, her definition including a bit more than Philip had thought to imagine. Within just days of coming home with Philip, Ginny found a little cat in a vacant lot. Hurt and hungry, the small animal sorrowfully meowed for help. Ginny understood the language of loneliness and hunger. Racing home to get Philip, the dog led her new best friend back to the scrawny little cat. She watched in relieved delight as Philip cornered the scared little creature, then picked her up and tucked her into his arm. Ginny cantered at Philip's side as the three of them headed for home. Next, Ginny discovered five kittens stuck in a narrow pipe on a building site. Then, a cat trapped in a box of broken glass at a window factory. And since then, Ginny has rescued literally hundreds of other stray cats!

Why this dedicated drive to serve and rescue felines? Perhaps the kitties somehow remind Ginny of the puppies she still misses, their sorrowful cries of pain and hunger reminding her of the days when her puppies yipped in a hunger she couldn't satisfy. Then again, perhaps Ginny is "rescuing" in answer to the vows between she and Philip at the animal shelter that day—and it includes his rescue from loneliness and boredom. Certainly the man who can no longer return to his job because of his disability has found new work, and purpose! Whatever the impetus or source, Ginny counts on the help of her best friend coming through for her.

They are a productive team. Ginny finds and rescues stray kittens and cats. (To date she has rescued some four hundred stray cats from the dangers and deprivation that come with homelessness!) It's Philip's job to look for homes for them and to seek donations to help cover the cost of health care and the food that he delivers to fourteen different sites each week.

Philip and Ginny's new line of work has been rewarding personally—and publicly. On November 21, 1998, ten-year-old Ginny-the-dog was named Cat-of-the-Year by the Westchester Feline Club! The publicity has served them well. Costarring in a full schedule of appearances, dog and man visit children in hospitals, ride in parades, and appear at ribbon cuttings and fundraising events. When they aren't playing celebrities, they are busy visiting local schools to promote spaying and neutering and to educate the public about protecting and caring for our furry friends.

Ginny and Philip. Each giving their love and in return getting the love they longed for. The hard times that brought Ginny and Philip together have long since been transformed to meaningful times resulting in the pearl of companionship and shared purpose. And, their bond of friendship is a lifeline to countless cats and kittens in need of rescue. Yet, for the heroic pooch and her devoted guardian, their fondness for each other is based on a simple principle: Loving and serving one another not only staves off loneliness and despair—but offers proof that we are all interdependent on one another. And there is an even bigger truth here: Giving love when you are without it becomes the most potent form of peace—in our homes, our communities, and in the world.

Separate Losses, Separate Dance

"Where there is sorrow, there is Holy Ground."
—OSCAR WILDE

Rabbi Wayne Dosick is fond of telling the parable of a delicate little bird who found shelter every day in the withered branches of a dried-up old tree in the middle of a deserted plain. One day, a whirlwind came and uprooted the tree. The tiny bird was forced to fly hundreds of miles in search of new shelter. . . .

Like the homeless little bird, Dr. Dosick would have his own whirlwind of tragedy uproot his life . . . and he, too, would be without shelter.

Standing before the ashes and charred remains of what had been his home, Wayne Dosick wailed aloud, the agonized cry wrenched from his heart. His wife, Ellen, stood beside him, her arms wrapped around her stomach as if to ward off the truth of it. Weeping softly, she shook her head, murmuring, "I can't believe it. I just can't believe it. Our beautiful home, all our beautiful things."

Only hours before they had stepped off an airplane, certain their lives were filled with security, laughter, and material possessions. Returning from their trip to celebrate the bar mitzvah of a dear friend's son, they couldn't have known that while they were gone, a wildfire had called for the evacuation of all the homes in their neighborhood. Now, standing before the smoldering ruins in tears, Wayne and Ellen numbly reached out to hold each other. The fire had burned their home to the ground and devoured *everything* they owned. Unable to fathom such an unexpected and destructive thief, Wayne uttered in disbelief, "Our lives will never be the same." He had no idea how comprehensive this statement would prove to be.

The couple's loss was magnified by the fact that both of them worked from home. Wayne, a rabbi, a writer and professor of Jewish studies at a university, wrote at home, as well as grading his students' papers there. Ellen, a spiritual psychotherapist, saw her clients and conducted workshops and seminars from home, in a section of the house she specifically designed for her work. Both their lives revolved around their house—and everything in it. Not only had they lost their beautiful nest and all of their personal valuables, but their offices along with all their professional valuables, as well. When their house sitter was ordered to immediately evacuate the home, she'd dashed through the house gathering up the family pets, then the Torah scroll and the hard drives from Wayne and Ellen's computers. She hadn't had time to pack up anything else and couldn't have known for certain what items were most important to Wayne and Ellen. Now, aside from those belongings that she'd rescued, all Wayne and Ellen owned were the clothes packed in their suitcases.

On the drive to Wayne's parents' house, where they would now stay, their grief and tears flowed as they began an inventory of all that had been lost. Each entry was accompanied by a dazed reality of the extent of that list. "All my books," Wayne murmured, speaking of the six thousand volumes in his rabbinic library. "They're irreplaceable," he moaned, referring to so many of the historic editions he had collected over the years. Then, remembering a literally priceless book, he blurted, "The Hebrew Bible!" The historic treasure had been saved from the fire of the Holocaust—but not an indiscriminate California wildfire.

"All our pictures," Ellen said softly, unable to comprehend the loss of mementos as important and irreplaceable as all their photos—from birth to present—of children growing up. Pictures of long deceased grandparents and great-grandparents, of special occasions, birthdays, the children receiving various awards, as well as the many precious times she and Wayne had shared, were lost forever—along with so many family valuables. Sadly, Ellen continued her growing account of their devastation, "The children's first baby shoes, my grandmother's Mother's Day ring, my aunt's gold watch." It was a *very* long list.

"My grandfather's pocket watch," Wayne added, his voice lowering to a new level of sorrow, remembering yet other family heirlooms passed down with love—and priceless in sentiment. There was a hundred-year-old grand piano, which had been in Ellen's family since she was a child, and Wayne's grandfather's prayer shawl. Besides these things, there were their more recent treasures: the watch Wayne received from his parents the day he was ordained, the pair of candlesticks Ellen was given on her bat mitzvah. There were quality pieces of art, collected with care and appreciation. All were gone. Every sermon Wayne had ever written, his rabbinic diploma, Ellen's client records, all the class notes from every class either of them had ever taught, tapes of radio shows Wayne had hosted, all their financial records and legal documents. The list of losses was endless. "How much is the Hermitage in St. Petersburg, Russia, worth?" a reporter once asked a guard at the palatial, world-famous museum. "It's impossible to ever know," came the guard's response. Now appraising their losses, that was exactly how Wayne and Ellen felt.

Tossing and turning in the guest room of Wayne's parents' home, all that was gone paraded through their minds, robbing them of sleep's escape. With each memory of yet another cherished possession forever lost, their hearts broke a little more. Finally, when there were no pieces left to break, Wayne and Ellen moved from feeling paralyzed by their plight to demanding "answers."

While reason and an eerie misery told Wayne and Ellen it was really true, part of them was not able to digest the depth and breadth of the chasm the fire left in their lives and so they viewed it from a distant, yet pained place of "why?" They took on God first. "Why me, God?" Wayne wondered. "What did I do to deserve this? How could you let this happen?" Ellen wagered her own inquisition. "Why would God be so unfair? How could a God we have faith in—one who watches over and protects—bring so much pain our way? Where is God when we need God most?"

God wasn't the only one they questioned. Other than the homes in their surrounding neighborhood, no one else had to deal with the horrific experience they had. Everywhere they went other people were happy and going on about their business. Why not? They hadn't suffered the losses that Wayne and Ellen had—some didn't even know of it. "Does anyone care about *us*?" they wondered. They questioned whether or not others would offer help in the work of rebuilding that lay ahead—or would heartfelt sympathy be all they were offered?

Immediately, any questions they had about whether or not people really cared about them, or about the warmth and charity of the human spirit, were answered. Not only could Wayne and Ellen readily see the loving support of family and friends, even caring strangers rallied to help them and others like them who had lost their homes. The Red Cross provided the first relief, followed by local charities. But it was the outpouring of ordinary people who offered extraordinary kindness that seemed most divinely orchestrated. For example, a group of ten- and eleven-year-old boys in their neighborhood, whose homes had survived the fire, took up a collection (raising three hundred dollars) to purchase tools to help them dig through the ashes. Then the boys asked the manager of the store if the tools might be delivered to the site where needed. The store manager was so impressed by the boys' thoughtfulness that he announced what the youths had done over the store's intercom, pledging he would match donations collected within the hour. Store patrons opened their hearts and their wallets. Nearly one thousand dollars worth of merchandise—gloves, rakes, shovels, and tools—were delivered at the site of the ruins the next morning.

Many others helped, too. Neighbors bought wood and wire screening and made large sifters, which they gave to those whose homes had been burned. Wayne's teaching colleagues took up a collection, and so did some of the university students. Checks from a variety of emergency funds from around the country came pouring in. Caring individuals from neighboring communities donated food, drinks, and flowers, and many willingly labored in the rubble beside Wayne,

Ellen, and the other victims of the wildfire. People did care —
and showed that they cared.

As they worked on restoring order in their daily lives,
picking up the broken pieces of their outer world, a different
crack surfaced, this one in the walls of their marriage. In the
wake of the fire and its losses, each of them was grieving their
own loss, each caught up in his or her own feelings. Wayne
grieved most for historic items — those irreplaceable symbols
of sentiment and connection through the ages; while Ellen
longed most for all their aesthetically beautiful things — those
she had so lovingly gathered together to make her house a
home. Throughout their marriage when Wayne needed emotional caretaking or felt harried or fragile, Ellen was there for
him, just as he was there for her when she needed his care.
Now they both "needed." Filled with their individual pain and
sorrow, consumed by their own feelings and needs, there
remained precious little ability to console the other.

The realization that they were not as united as they once
thought was frightening. It was a lonely feeling — and very dis-
comforting. Filled with sorrow and a sense of utter discon-
nection, they slowly began to drift apart. They found
themselves lashing out in frustration or breaking apart in
anger. Sometimes they clung to each other, other times they
needed distance and slept in separate rooms. Sometimes they
were powerfully drawn together, and other times they considered separating so that they each might heal in their own way
without imposing their needs on the other.

Other differences loomed between them. They had different ways of dealing with their grief. One needed silence and
aloneness, the other to talk and be physically close. Ellen
wanted to act immediately and move into a rental that was
similar in size and as near to their former home as possible.

She wanted to carry on with life and return as quickly as possible to some semblance of normalcy. Wayne wanted to "mourn in a cocoon" and wanted nothing to do with rebuilding on the same site—where a mere glance at the vicinity of their "once-home" held the power to reignite the blaze of pain within him.

Even their need to understand and reconcile was different. Ellen was content to let understanding unfold in its own good time, to let God and the universe enlighten them as they would. Wayne wanted immediate answers. He needed to make sense of what was happening to their lives, to their closeness right now, and felt he couldn't move forward until this closeness was restored.

Five decades of their lives reduced to ashes, and now the bigger meltdown looked to be the demise of their relationship. They were surprised—and alarmed—that their marriage seemed so fragile, so transparent. Did the voice of their agony have to do with the crisis of their loss or the health and happiness of their marriage? Wondering if their marriage would survive the fire, they asked, "Do we want to be together, or is this marriage over?"

They began with a discussion of their commitment to each other. They realized the strain of coping with their loss could draw them apart—and yet, they were *good* friends and respected and trusted each other. This was the foundation on which their marriage had been built. They wanted their marriage to go on—and now it, too, required rebuilding. They loved each other and had chosen to be together. Regardless of the magnitude of their outer loss, in the midst of being fragile, vulnerable, and each in need themselves, the couple realized they also needed to care about each other.

And so in the months that followed, Ellen and Wayne engaged in a cautious dance. Sometimes this called for talking and listening to each other; other times they needed silence to process their own thoughts and feelings. Their renewed commitment nourished compassion for each other, one in which each was able to step outside of himself—even if just for small spaces of time—and tune in to the needs of the other. This perspective made all the difference in the world. They concluded it was *okay* to grieve differently and that it was okay to grieve separately. Their differences didn't mean that they didn't love each other, nor that either deemed or valued his own anguish as being greater. After all, who can say which is better: to cry inconsolably or mourn silently? Which is a greater loss: that of a rare Hebrew Bible or that of a statue carefully chosen to grace your home? There's no way to measure these losses or establish a hierarchy to their importance in the heart.

Now a new layer of healing was made possible. Aware that there were so many colliding feelings going on inside each of them, Wayne and Ellen decided not to make any major decisions while their grief was raw unless doing so was absolutely necessary. They focused on the tasks that were at hand: selecting a rental, re-establishing their work patterns, going about the duties of day-to-day life. And, concluding that God didn't want them to suffer, nor had He deserted them, they made their peace. God was there with them through the pain. In fact, in the wake of the anguish of their loss, it was their faith that granted them respite from the pain of the ordeal and instilled the courage and hope needed to rebuild their lives. This faith allowed them to renew their commitment to each other, enabling them to be compassionate and supportive of one another. United, they returned to the work of restoring their outer world.

The parable of the little bird has a happy ending, and so does the story of this couple. Forced to fly hundreds of miles in search of new shelter, the delicate little bird came upon a lush forest, full of fruit-laden trees.

Life looks better for Wayne and Ellen, too. It's safe to say they're on the other side of the devastating grief caused by the wildfire. They no longer look back and question "why?"; they look forward and ask "how?" They are busy rebuilding and attending to their professional lives and have renewed their love and vibrancy for their lives as a couple.

Wayne had been right, their lives would never be the same. They were to be so much *more*—most especially for Wayne himself. The indiscriminate wildfire would force Dr. Dosick— a "man of God," a renowned rabbi, his very life dedicated to his faith—to fly deeper within his own soul in search of the full breadth and scope of faith in God. His faith had literally been tested and tried by fire. Like the little bird, Dr. Dosick, too, found a lush forest: a faith greater than he had ever known, one that had gone from *concept* to *experience*, which profoundly deepened his sense of God. The branches of his earlier faith withered in comparison.

Through experience Wayne *learned* what he already knew. A faith once rooted in his intellectual and professional life now flourishes in his heart and nests comfortably in his soul. His suffering led him to a deeper understanding of God. This understanding is the pearl he now offers his congregation in *their* times of need.

Searching Seattle

"Courage is the price that life exacts for granting peace."
—AMELIA EARHART

"Adopted," they had said. The word held more sting than riding the bus with two rowdy brothers who teased and taunted and wouldn't stick up for her. It was worse than having twin sisters who were like peas in a pod and didn't much want her company. It was more humiliating than when the teacher called on her in class and she didn't have the right answer, so the entire class had laughed—but only after the teacher had given her a disappointed look. The pain was even more excruciating than wondering why she felt as if no one liked her. Now she had a reason for feeling so lonely—and it felt even worse than feeling lonely when you had no reason to feel lonely at all!

MaryBeth was but a vulnerable little girl of eleven when she learned that "her mother didn't want her." The news struck her with a devastating force, like an arrow piercing her heart. Already she felt forsaken. Even in a crowded family of two brothers and twin sisters, young MaryBeth felt alone, always the baby, the last one chosen, the odd man out. And now, she learned she really was a stray! Everyone had someone except MaryBeth. Her parents had each other, her brothers had each other, her twin sisters had each other. There were no pair-bondings for MaryBeth—not even a pet to cradle and cuddle. Now this—she was "adopted." So that was why she had sandy-colored hair and green eyes while her two brothers and two sisters had dark hair and dark eyes. Now, it all made sense! None of them belonged to her! Not even the two adults she'd thought were her parents!

Over time, the little girl became certain if she could only meet her "real" mother, her life would be better. If only she could see her, hear her, touch her. Be with her. *"Mommy,"* the deserted young child cried silently, *"I don't know why you left me, and I don't know where you are, but I'm a really good girl and I know you'd like me. Nobody here likes me. Wherever you are, please come get me."*

The curious little girl asked if she might have "just a little visit with her mother." But her parents maintained they knew nothing about the whereabouts of the woman who "abandoned" her. They informed her *they* were her parents, her family—and she should be happy and grateful she had them and her sisters and brothers and a home. And that was that—case closed. No further nonsense of wanting to know more of her "biological" parents would be tolerated. She was harshly disciplined as it was; when her parents discovered she shed tears because she was "missing Mommy," she was chastised even more. Crushed, the melancholy youngster learned to keep her longings to herself—and vowed that one day she *would* find her mother.

That her mother "gave her up" saddened her and made her feel discarded. Being a young child—who felt disconnected from the family she had somehow become a part of, feeling like an unwelcomed guest—the little girl created a fantasy of the loving mother for whom she longed. Included in the profile of a very beautiful, gentle, and loving woman was a very logical explanation for her mother's absence. Obviously robbers had come to their house to steal their beautiful possessions and had taken *her* very beautiful mother with them. She was but an infant and her mother had hidden her in a closet so they wouldn't find and steal her baby, too. But they had taken her mother and so it was up to MaryBeth to get her mother back. And one day, she would find her mother and rescue her.

The little girl played out this search and rescue time and time again. It was just a matter of her growing bigger and being able to get away from this family who held her captive. In the meantime, the rescue loomed like gnawing hunger pains always rumbling with an appetite, wanting, needing to be fed. The desire to find her mother grew hungrier with each passing year. *"Mommy,"* the determined child cried silently, *"Wherever you are, I'll save you. I'll find you."*

As a feisty adolescent, MaryBeth began an *active* secret search for her mother. Shrouded in a great wall of secrecy, her search centered on how one goes about finding "lost family." Using the yellow pages in the counselor's office at school and in the homes of friends, MaryBeth searched for adoption agencies and ways to get information about one's "past." All her efforts proved futile.

She grew cynical of ever finding her birth mother. And so she called off the search.

But at twenty-nine, married and the mother of three children, the lonely ache in her heart intensified even more. She desperately wanted to meet and know the woman who had brought her into the world. And, she wanted her children to know their grandmother and their ancestry. Moreover, the love she felt for her own children gave her a new understanding and a deeper compassion for the kind of love and pain inherent in giving up a child. Surely her mother was missing her too, but was helpless to do anything about it, as she had been all these years. And so she reopened her promise to rescue her mother and to reunite them.

Although she launched a full-scale search, dead ends were a constant. The courts refused to release confidential information. Agencies and private investigators all required fees she couldn't afford to pay. Disappointed but undaunted, MaryBeth continued casting about leaving nothing to chance. She made it easier for her mother to find her—doing things like having her maiden name listed in the telephone book and restoring her adopted name (in addition to her married name) on all her legal records. This took some doing, but in searching for the whereabouts of her mother, MaryBeth realized how important these "clues" would be.

She also talked openly of her search to relatives and friends, always ready to consider their advice. Upon the suggestion of one friend, she bought a used computer to help in her search. Patiently teaching herself the ins and outs of its use, MaryBeth then got "on-line" where she discovered a wealth of adoption support groups and registries. Every night, the young mother of three tucked her children in bed, then went to her computer to continue her fervent search. Unfailingly, after logging on she checked the registry to see if anyone was searching for her. Quelling the twinge of disappointment she always felt when she found that no one was, MaryBeth would then "chat" with members of the various support groups. Sharing the common bond of being adopted and also searching for their birth parents as well, they offered her the comfort of understanding her frustration and yearning. Perhaps most important, in sharing their experiences and possible sources for finding missing parents, they provided MaryBeth with direction and encouragement. Several support group members urged her to contact many of the places she had previously called. "Try again!" they advised. "Public sympathy for a child's search for her natural parents is changing, along with the stigma of being an unwed mother (in case hers was), so stringent confidentiality policies are relaxing. Besides, state confidentiality laws—and personnel—change from time to time. You might get someone who will 'bend the rules' a little. Try again."

Following their advice, MaryBeth began by calling the Catholic adoption agency she had called on several occasions. This time, just as her "computer friends" had proposed, there was a breakthrough. "Alice" was much less hesitant than her predecessor, who had not only refused to give MaryBeth information about her past, but even about how she might go about counseling her children when they asked about their grandmother's side of the family.

Locating MaryBeth's file, Alice released details that were entirely new to MaryBeth. "Your birth name was Lisa Anne," she revealed. "Let me see what else I can let you know. . . . " MaryBeth could hear her turning the pages in the file, then she continued in hushed confidential tones, "Your mother's first name is Lucette."

"Lucette?" MaryBeth rolled the name over her tongue, savoring the sound as she repeated it aloud and wrote it down—a thoroughly superfluous action, since just hearing it seared the name into her heart like a branding iron—so she could never forget it. "She is French and she has a *very* French last name. I really wish I could tell you her last name, but it could cost me my job," Alice apologized, then offered up all the details of MaryBeth's mysterious past she was allowed to disclose under the new and reformed confidentiality laws. "She comes from a family of seven and was raised in the northern part of the state." MaryBeth devoured each new morsel, carefully digesting every added crumb of information and piecing together a trail that might lead to her mother. Then the clerk offered up an important piece of information: her mother's date of birth.

Fueled by these new facts, the possibility of finding her mother was more real than it had ever been. Pursuing the precious goal she had long sought, MaryBeth added eighteen years to her mother's date of birth and calculated the most probable year of her mother's graduation from high school. Making a list of every library in the northern part of the state, she called each and every one of them, asking the librarian if he or she could please run a check for any female seniors in the year she had calculated who had the first name of Lucette and "a French last name."

Several times a day for the next few days a clerk from each of the various libraries would call back to report they had found no such matching names. But on the third day, after MaryBeth assumed the search was over, a librarian called to tell MaryBeth she had found a possible match! Immediately, MaryBeth made plans to drive the seventy miles to the northern part of the state where the library was located to view the photograph in the yearbook.

Her heart thumping in anticipation, MaryBeth opened the yearbook to the page the librarian had marked for her. Her eyes scanned the pictures and names, then halted on the name she'd been given. She stared at the photo, and her stomach tightened with disappointment—MaryBeth just knew it *wasn't* her mother. Wondering if her mother's last name could be a more "common" French name, MaryBeth started at the beginning of the senior class and went through each picture, each name, carefully studying each face. When the search turned up no one who matched, she then did the same for the junior class, the sophomore class, the freshman class—closely examining each and every female—all to no avail.

Following a sleepless night after her defeat, to her surprise, yet another library called. They too had a student who could be a possible match—a senior with the first name of Lucette and a French last name of Devereaux. Again, MaryBeth drove to the library, this one three hours away, to view the photo. Taking a deep breath to steel herself for whatever the outcome, MaryBeth entered the library. Opening the yearbook, her eyes again made their hungry search, freezing on the name and photograph the librarian had indicated. Instant joy flooded her heart while its tears filled her eyes. As certainly as she knew the last photograph hadn't been her mother, MaryBeth knew this one *was* her mother! The young woman who gazed out at MaryBeth as she stared down at the photo, looked exactly like the young woman in her own graduation picture. In awe, MaryBeth studied every tiny characteristic and nuance of the eighteen-year-old in the yearbook. Trying to satisfy a hunger she'd known for so many years, she feasted greedily on the sight of her mother's features. The photo was black and white, but MaryBeth could see she and her mother had the same heart-shaped face, same arched brows and thick lashes, same high cheekbones and the same straight, delicate nose, the deeply cleft chin. MaryBeth marshaled her wildly elated emotions and jumbled thoughts, photocopied the picture of her mother and headed home. *"Mom! At last, I've found you! I can't wait to show you my children, Mom— your grandchildren. They're so cute. There's Amanda, she's seven . . . and Travis, four . . . and Glory, the baby. . . . "* All the way home MaryBeth talked out loud to the woman she had constructed as a child and now made revisions according to the picture she had seen in the high school yearbook — her "real" mother. Quiet only while drying her eyes and blowing her nose during breaks in her recurring bouts of tears, she chattered on and on as though her mother was in the seat next to her.

"I've found Mom!" she yelled to her husband, the minute she walked in the door, waving the treasured photocopy in front of him. Taking it in his hands, her husband looked at it and walked over to his wife's high school graduation picture on the nearby shelf. He took it down and held it next to the photo, searching one picture, then the other. "Wow," he breathed. "You really do look just like her — you look like your . . . mom." "Mom," he said, repeating the words tenderly as though the woman was his own mother — and then realized in a way, she was. Certainly he, too, was related to her. Tenderly he took his wife in his arms. His search, too, had ended.

MaryBeth's mother finally had a name — first and last — and a face.

The next day MaryBeth called the agency and once again asked for Alice, the compassionate woman who cleverly fed MaryBeth clues, those which could possibly reunite a daughter with her mother. Having received such promising direction, MaryBeth now wanted agency confirmation. She asked the social worker, "Is my mother's last name Devereaux?"

"Yes," Alice answered.

MaryBeth had found her true mother! Now she need but "rescue" her.

Early the next day, MaryBeth went to her local library and began her search of the telephone books covering the northern part of the state. *"Okay, Mom, give me a hand here,"* MaryBeth cajoled, happier than ever now that she felt "connected."

MaryBeth scrolled the names in one phone book, then another, then another, and yet another. As she fingered through the pages of each phone book, she tried to shrug away the nagging fear that her mother's name had no doubt changed through marriage. It was a tedious, monotonously detailed task—but not one that lost her interest for even a moment. Then, hours later MaryBeth found a Lucette Devereaux, and next to it, an address and telephone number! There it was, right in front of her eyes—so vivid, so definite, so long sought. MaryBeth could hardly believe what she was seeing. Struggling to still the small tremors of excitement in her hands, she copied down the phone number and address. She had a face—albeit one possessed in years past—now she stared at a phone number. *"Oh, please be you, Mom. Please be the right one!"* she whispered.

For all these years she wondered what her mother's voice would sound like. Now she would know. Still sitting in the library, she pulled her cell phone from her purse, her fingers fumbling as she dialed the number. She listened, her pulse quickening as the phone at the other end rang. "Hello?" a woman answered. Flustered, MaryBeth panicked at the sound of the woman's voice and wasn't able to say anything. When there was no response, Lucette Devereaux repeated, "Hello?" and several seconds later repeated yet again, "Hello?" Deluged by a crashing wave of sentiment, MaryBeth hurriedly punched the "end call" button. Tears filled her eyes and she could hardly see to find the off button on the phone. "Mom," she whispered, "you're real."

Even so, she didn't have the courage to call back.

The very next day, MaryBeth left her three children in the care of her husband and drove the thirty miles to where her mother lived. Her plan was to simply sit in the car by her mother's house and wait for her mother to come out. Hopefully, Lucette would go somewhere that day—maybe to the market to buy groceries. If she did, MaryBeth planned to follow her and watch her from a distance: see what her mother looked liked, how she walked, moved—as though these observations would somehow ease her into "getting to know her." The Saturday skies were clear except for an occasional cloud that drifted ever so slowly across the horizon, just like the unexplainable doubts that floated across MaryBeth's mind as she drove. If she followed her mother into a store, what would she do if she and her mother bumped into one another, such as in a shopping aisle in the store? Would she simply say "excuse me" and move on? Would she ask the woman, "Do I know you?" With every mile MaryBeth grew more and more apprehensive about how things would unfold.

Several times she stopped to ask for directions, each time adding information to her hand-drawn map. Locating the street where the mother she had been wanting to be with for nearly two decades lived, MaryBeth grew nervous and drove down the streets that surrounded the one on which her mother lived. And then, finally having the courage to find the house, she turned onto the street. Scrutinizing the address on the paper in her hand and then the addresses marked on the mailboxes, MaryBeth located her mother's house and then drove slowly by it—several times. So this was her mother's house. Anxious about what she should do now, Lucette's daughter drove two houses down the street, pulled over, parking at the curb facing the house. There she simply sat in the car, tending to resting her racing heart and composing her thoughts. Hopeful, she watched the house closely for any signs of her mother.

Three hours of such vigilant waiting and still not a single sign of her mother. She studied the house as if it were the pyramid that held all the precious mysteries of her life within its walls. *"Should I knock on the door?"* she wondered, but instead took out her cellular phone and dialed the number.

"Hello?" a woman answered on the second ring.

MaryBeth ventured: "Is this Lucette Devereaux?"

"Yes," the woman replied.

Her heart bursting into a runaway gallop, her breathing all but arrested, MaryBeth considered hanging up, but she'd already done that once to the poor woman. Besides, she'd come much too far for that now. "You don't know me," she said, trying to find her breath, "but my name is MaryBeth and I was born on November 8, 1965. My birth name was Lisa Anne."

The woman at the other end of the line let out a little gasp, the sweetest sound MaryBeth could imagine. This was followed by a dazed pause, and then, unable to do more than whisper, the woman appealed, "Could you repeat that?"

"I was born on November 8, 1965. The name you gave me was Lisa Anne," MaryBeth said again, wiping away the tears trickling from the corner of her eyes.

"Oh, my!" the woman said. "My baby . . . my lost baby girl . . . " Lucette Devereaux's pause was a full, painful silence, one that spoke the same longing her daughter also knew so well. "Are you all right?" her mother finally asked with instinctive maternal concern and then continued, "I didn't think I would ever hear from you! I tried to find you when you were in high school and again when you turned eighteen. They wouldn't help me and said I was being selfish and should be ashamed for wanting to disrupt your life, that you were happy with a family of brothers and sisters . . . so I, so I didn't . . . " Sobbing, she added, "I thought I'd lost you forever."

The phone pressed to her ear, MaryBeth literally shook with small sobs of joy and remnants of mourning for the years she'd lost with her heart's most precious link to life—her mother. "What, what . . . do I say now?" her mother stammered.

"I don't know what to say either," MaryBeth admitted, crying and at a loss to think clearly. "I guess I could write. Would you like that?"

"Yes, yes—write. Please write," her mother implored.

Pulling in an unsteady breath, MaryBeth closed her eyes a moment and then swallowed. "I can go *home* and write to you or I can come to your house—*right now*," the hopeful daughter blurted, hoping her mother wouldn't feel ambushed by this sudden approach.

"My house?" her mother parroted, obviously stunned. "Can you repeat that?"

"I'm parked down the street," her voice whimpered.

"*Here?*" the woman's voice cracked, as she began to weep again. "You're here?" Shedding years of pent-up longing, mother and daughter both cried into the phone, knowing it was safe to let their feelings flow freely. "Please come," her mother whispered and then pleaded, "please come."

MaryBeth was barely out of the car when she saw her mother hurrying down the steps, frantically searching the street in both directions for her daughter. MaryBeth looked at the woman besieged with tears, her mouth quivering so much she raised her hand to try and still it—only to find her hand shuddered with the same unruly flutters. Their hearts engulfed with emotion, eagerly the women approached each other and simply embraced one another. Drawing back, they studied each other's beloved yet unknown faces—so familiar yet unfamiliar. The eyes—their shape, their color, the daintily heart-shaped narrow lips, the cleft chins. "You're so beautiful," the mother whispered. "You are, too," the daughter said in return. Lifting a hand that still trembled to smooth her daughter's hair, she tried to explain. "I was sixteen, pregnant, and unwed. Your father was a serviceman home on furlough." Tears streamed down her face. "He never even knew he had fathered you," she said, apologizing over and over. "My parents insisted that I give you up for adoption . . . but I . . . " Perhaps thinking her words were too soon, she stopped and simply basked in the sight of the daughter she had unwillingly given up, an act that had cast a dark and oppressive shadow on every day of her life since. "I thought I'd lost you," her mother cried softly, still drinking in the sight of her daughter.

"I knew I'd find you," MaryBeth whispered through her tears. "It's been such a long search . . . but I always *knew* I'd come to your rescue . . . our rescue."

However we understand or speak the mystery of the family ties that bind one heart to another, it is a bond that not even years and distance can forget. Perhaps it is etched into the soul's memory, one we can never erase. Certainly this was true for MaryBeth and her mother, wherein once again the human spirit had prevailed using the dialog of heartache and longing to drive the search to connect two hearts missing each other— one having given life to the other. Today mother and daughter live happily and fully in each other's lives, both hearts appeased now that the durable and treasured pearl of family, having been lost for so long, has been reconnected.

No Expiration Date on Love

> "There are years that ask questions, and years
> that answer."
>
> — ZORA NEALE HURSTON

Hearing the wail of a siren, Paul looked in his rearview mirror and saw the flashing lights of a police car signaling him to pull over. "Oh, great," the forty-eight-year-old groaned, glancing down at his speedometer. Seeing that he was traveling at a legal speed, he tried to recall whether he could have missed a stop sign, but he was certain there had been no stop signs. "What's this about?" he grumbled under his breath. Then it dawned on him that the tags on the license plate of his friend's car, which he was driving, were expired. "Damn!" he muttered.

Behind Paul, LAPD officer Kelly Benitez eyed the black Thunderbird with suspicion as it slowed down to pull over. His shift was almost over and he could have let another officer follow up on the car for him, but *something* about that black Thunderbird wouldn't let him do that. Immediately noticing the driver's lapsed tags, the twenty-nine-year-old officer radioed dispatch and had them run a check on the plates. The vehicle wasn't stolen. Still, Officer Benitez couldn't shrug off his curiosity about whatever it was that compelled him to further investigate this driver.

Officer Benitez stopped behind the car that had pulled off the highway and walked to the driver's window. "May I see your driver's license, vehicle registration, and proof of insurance, please?" he asked rotely. Paul, a local schoolteacher, considered apologizing, explaining it was a friend's car and she had the tags but just hadn't gotten around to putting them on. Instead, he simply handed the officer his license, registration, and proof of insurance—then waited for the citation he knew was coming.

Officer Benitez took the documents and automatically scanned them—the driver's license wasn't expired, the photograph on it matched the face of the driver, there were no driving restrictions listed. But then, when the officer saw the man's name on the driver's license, chills ran up his spine and his heart began to pound wildly. Taking a closer look at the photo on the license and then a closer look at the man in the car—dark eyes, dark complexion, the tilt of his eyebrows, the shape of his nose and eyes—the officer realized this was *not* just another routine traffic check. Gut instinct told him he may well have come upon the target of a manhunt he'd been tracking for years. Trying to sound as casual as he could with his emotions under siege, Officer Benitez began to question the man about where he had lived years before, people he might have known, whether or not he'd been drafted.

The motorist *had* been drafted. Paul was but a teenager then—one who left behind a four-month-old son. The young father had seen his little boy only once. The newly inducted soldier and the boy's mother never married, and after that one visit, the overwhelmed teen never saw either her or his son again. He was active military and had been transferred several times; she had married and taken a new last name. Having been adopted, her family history was so sketchy that he was unable to find her. Losing track of his son was a travesty the regret-filled father could never forget—nor had he ever forgiven himself for it. Even after his marriage years later and most especially with the birth of another child, Paul's urgent aching for his missing boy lingered. He had searched, but to no avail. The absence of his son left a painful void within him—always lurking in the backdrop of his daily life.

Although Officer Kelly Benitez considered himself happy in life, he too knew a certain void. He had never completely allayed the vague ache within that pined for the father he never knew. It wasn't the loss of a father to play ball with when he was growing up that made him feel most empty. He wasn't without a "male role model"—he had his maternal grandfather in his life. It was just that he longed to become the son to the father he knew in his heart. And he was curious to know about his paternal family heritage. What did his father look like? Was he tall or short—or was he of medium height? What was the tone in his voice—was it deep and gravelly or gentle or soft-spoken? What kind of a man was he? Did he have a gentle nature or was he a boisterous, brusque man? Did he have a sense of humor or was he more on the serious side? Was he playful? Was he musical? Was he an athlete? What did he do for work? Was he an officer in the navy, a truck-driver, a politician? What were his beliefs on politics, religion, the arts, and life in general? Was his father single or married? Did Kelly have brothers or sisters? Kelly wanted to know the answers to these questions—and a million others.

The absent data made him feel like a part of him was missing, like there was a lost piece of the puzzle of his identity, a critical facet that left the otherwise complete man incomplete.

What wasn't missing was the sense that, even though not present physically in his life, his father loved him. At least this was the feeling his heart offered up each time Kelly looked at the cherished photo taken with his father when he was four months old—the only photo ever taken of the two of them together. While too young to actually remember this occasion, Kelly had assigned a happy life to the family of two in the photo. The scene it depicted was his youthful father, clean-cut and dressed in his military uniform, proudly holding him, a baby dressed in a white and blue outfit, innocently oblivious to the importance of the occasion. In the photo, his father wrapped both arms tightly around him to cuddle him close yet high on his chest, as he beamed with paternal pride—and love. This picture was more precious than anything else Kelly owned and sat framed on a shelf where he could view it *every* day of his life. And whenever that "missing piece" of his heart began to throb with a painful yearning, Kelly would look at this photo. Seeing their togetherness in that picture somehow brought them together again.

Even so, both his heart and that priceless photo were constant reminders of his longing to know his father. It was a relentless ache, one with a voice and a life all its own—one that had been with him all his life. His was a heart that simply *refused* to let go of his father.

Suddenly more captivated than irritated, Paul frowned in perplexed fascination as he answered the officer's puzzling questions. Now it was Paul who felt a growing sense of peculiarity and déjà vu. He closely scanned the officer's face, then looked down at the last name on the officer's badge—and then up at the officer. *"Could it be?"* he wondered in disbelief.

Magnetically, their dark eyes locked, searching each other's faces. In that instant, it all clicked. Both men intuitively *knew* they were father and son! Each held the missing piece for the two souls who had been separated by circumstances so long ago. "*You* are Kelly," Paul whispered, almost speechless. Kelly mutely nodded, then answered a stunned "Yes!"

Exhilarated, yet in a state of shock, Paul exuberantly stuck his hand out the window, and still so dumbfounded he could barely utter the words, announced, "*I'm* your dad." Instantly tossing his citation pad on the roof of the car, Kelly clasped his father's hands in both of his, then hastily opened the car door. His father clamored from the car and threw his arms around his son. "My son," he choked, tears streaming down his face. "My son," he repeated, stroking his son's back as he embraced him. "There hasn't . . . there hasn't been a day that's gone by that I haven't thought of you!"

Filled with an excitement and wonder they could barely contain, the reunited father and son drove to the police station where Kelly worked, so that he could end his shift and they could talk. Sitting at Kelly's desk, neither of them seemed able to get enough of the other. There was so much to cover, each wanting to know all they could—details both trivial and important. They were absolutely amazed to discover that although they'd been separated twenty-nine years and lived many states apart, they now lived only five miles away from each other! Yet, the detail each man clung to most dearly was the discovery that each shared a deep and unwavering desire to find the other—for all these years.

As they prepared to leave the station that day, Paul took in one last proud drink of all the details of his son's work environment. Scanning his beloved son's desk, Paul's gaze froze when he saw the words on a to-do list that sat on its blotter: 1) Make dental appointment; 2) Schedule tune-up with

mechanic; 3) Mail insurance payment . . . the list continued. . .
But it was entry six that had seized his attention and his heart.
It read: *6) Find my father.*

And Kelly Benitez had.

Glancing tenderly at his son, Paul then leaned over the
desk, picked up a pen, and drew a line through number six on
the to-do list. With tears in his eyes, he looked up at his son,
nodded, and said, "That one's done." Reverently, the two men
silently left the station, arm in arm, their lives changed forever.

Two men traveling about their day, each with a deep, if
hidden, desire to find the other in a city of millions. And then,
one day, as if orchestrated by divine intervention, their paths
collide and they are reunited. If we watch closely, and most
especially if we are looking for them, we will find that syn-
chronicities manifest often in our lives. Finding them can be as
simple as listening to the call within or following up on a tip
whispering within the heart—or even driving a car with
expired tags!

Sometimes fate takes a heavy hand in life and literally
hands us the pearl! This is most always the case for those who
sincerely *believe*; for the heart diligently wills wishes into being.
Blessings are bestowed upon the spirit that has total faith that
the universe in its infinite wisdom delivers to its children love
in its most profound incarnations.

Phoenix Rising

*"One does not discover new lands without consenting
to lose sight of the shore for a very long time."*
—ANDRÉ GIDE

I was making my way through the crowd at the
annual American Booksellers Association, when
suddenly my attention was eerily drawn by an almost mag-
netic energy at my right. Looking over in that direction, I
saw a lithe, feminine young woman in a regal, cherry-red suit,
sitting at a small, round table, autographing books. She sat
erect, proud, and yet, her demeanor was poised and inviting.
A long line of people, all holding a book, stood waiting to
meet her. Taking stock of her surroundings, the lovely
woman in black patent stilettos—her legs crossed
demurely at the ankles—looked over the crowd, her lustrous, shoulder-length curls—the color of summer
wheat—swaying as she turned her head from side to
side. She was, on all accounts, a breathtaking sight.

As though she could feel my eyes upon her, the intriguing woman with the cat-shaped eyes lifted her head and seized my stare. They were masterful eyes: commanding, yet playful; guarded, yet content. She then flashed a sweet and genuine smile—as though we were dear friends. I didn't know her from Adam other than she was an author who, like me, had been invited by the publishers to autograph copies of her latest book for bookstore buyers at the convention. Quite sure she didn't know me, I returned her smile and continued on my way.

I hadn't taken but three or four steps when I was again drawn to look at the radiant woman. As if she could sense my eyes on her, once again she looked up from her autographing and without searching the crowd, looked directly at me. By now, I was within a few feet of her. To her smile she added the quietly spoken words, "You must give a copy of my book to my sister."

Her sister? Did I know her sister? I didn't know this woman—certainly I'd remember this vision of a woman who looked like a starlet and had the presence of Mother Teresa—but perhaps I did know her sister. Perhaps that was why she was friendly with me, or perhaps I reminded her of someone and this was a case of mistaken identity. Then again, maybe her words weren't intended for me at all, but rather, someone in the crowd who stood near me. If I looked puzzled, she didn't notice. She smiled sweetly, lowered her head, and continued to sign autographs. Just minutes away from my own autographing session, I hurried along.

Nearly an hour-and-a-half later, my own book-signing almost over, I looked up to see how many people might still be waiting in line for me. There, over to the side, I noticed the striking woman in the exquisite cherry-red suit, waiting patiently. When I had finally signed the last book, she came over. Holding up a copy of her book, her beautiful smile once again lighting up her face, she informed me, "I brought you a book for my sister."

"Your sister?" I prodded, hoping she'd take the lead and refresh my memory.

"Your daughter," the mystery woman said simply. "This book is for your daughter. She's going through a tough moment in her life, and I want her to know she's courageous and loved."

"You know my daughter?" I asked, now more perplexed than ever. Casually, I glanced at her suit jacket for a name tag like the one I had on, but she wasn't wearing one. Who was this "familiar" woman? And my daughter wasn't going through a tough time, in fact, she was in a "good place." Allowing her actions to speak for her, the woman opened the book and inscribed, "We are all sisters. Keep the faith. Everything happens for a reason. God has a plan. He's just 'working it.' Your sister, RaNelle."

Seeing her use of the word "sister" resolved at least a little of the mystery about whom she had meant. "How did you know I have a daughter?" I questioned.

"I see the love of a parent in your face," she said, "one who is looking through the hopeful eyes of a mother."

"Have we met before?" I asked, but somehow I knew the question was rhetorical. Even if I hadn't met her before, her very presence was so powerfully spirited and loving, she needed no invitation to be my friend.

"I'm RaNelle. RaNelle Wallace," she said sweetly, extending her hand to me.

It was then that I noticed that scars covered nearly every inch of her visible skin.

Though it's difficult to move beyond her soulful presence, there is yet another reality to RaNelle Wallace. Hers is a gripping story of the tenacity and majesty of the boundless human spirit—a living human phoenix having risen from the ashes, emerging a more glorious bird than before. And yet, the "before bird" was pretty exquisite, too.

She was beautiful and young, with bright eyes and flawless complexion, angelic features and armed with a quick wit and a vivacious personality. Married and the mother of two small children, RaNelle Wallace was, in the words of those who knew her, "a package." And a most talented one. With a degree in communications and a promising internship at a local television station, her professional future looked bright. Her dreams were to anchor the news—at even bigger and more prestigious television stations. She appeared to be on her way towards living those dreams. What more could she possibly want?

A little more happiness in her marriage for one thing. High school sweethearts, she and Terry had married right out of high school. Though volatile from the beginning, their home life had become intolerable. They'd been to marriage counseling, but it didn't seem to curtail their constant cycles of bitter bickering and long stretches of icy silence. When Terry said he wanted to explore making a career move to Utah, their marriage counselor suggested that the couple take the trip together—without the children. Perhaps a little time alone would help them resolve a few things and bring them closer together—perhaps rekindle their passion. And so they made plans to fly to Salt Lake City and rent a car for the drive up to Park City where they would look into jobs, schools, and housing.

But the trip hadn't been the second honeymoon RaNelle had hoped for, nor had it been a rekindling spark for the relationship. In fact, the couple concluded they just weren't in love anymore. Bound for home, RaNelle and her husband boarded the family's single-engine airplane with the knowledge their marriage was now over. But in addition to the feelings of discomfort and defeat looming between them because of that resolution, there was another frustration stalking RaNelle. Even before she had gone on this trip, she'd been haunted by a strange sense of foreboding about flying. Over and over, she'd experienced what felt like premonitions of doom, a quiet inner voice telling her not to board the plane. Now the voice was practically roaring. But she wasn't sure who the voice belonged to: Was it her instincts or her broken heart?

Her premonitions of doom were valid. Less than thirty minutes into the flight, bad weather caused zero visibility and the aircraft suddenly crashed into a mountainside. Careening off the tops of some boulders and slamming into the sides of others, the plane's belly was ripped open on the jagged rocks and it came to a halt with its nose and left side just inches from a rock wall. RaNelle heaved a pent-up breath of terrified relief. The plane had crashed, but she and Terry had survived! But her moment of relief was snatched away by the sight of the flames spreading from the bottom of the fuselage and now lashing hungrily towards them. "Open the door!" Terry shouted from his seat across from her, knowing it was the only door from which they could escape. As RaNelle struggled to get the jammed door open, the smell of gasoline fumes and the sensation of intense heat engulfed her. Frantically she kicked at the door until finally it flung open. Fresh air gushed into the plane igniting with the fumes, turning their small craft into a raging inferno. Suddenly, a burst of heat, like a blow torch, threw RaNelle from the plane. In the same instant, flames attacked her and ate at her face and body. She raised her hands to her face in an attempt to beat out the flames, only to discover that skin was hanging from both of them. Pain consumed her, and she felt certain she would die—then suddenly, a squall of snow and slush whipped over her, extinguishing the flames. But as quickly as the wind came up, it stilled and so the squall died. Waves of nausea and pain buckled her. RaNelle was in critical condition—and she knew it. She was hanging onto life by a mere thread of willpower.

Still, she and Terry were alive!

And yet, their ordeal had only begun. Now they had to get down off the mountain—a five-mile trek—and get help. Because Terry's hands were badly burned, he could neither carry nor physically support RaNelle in getting down the mountain. So instead, for two hours—hours that felt like an eternity to RaNelle—her husband coaxed and prodded her to put one foot in front of the other . . . one foot in front of the other . . . until at last they reached a highway where they managed to flag down help.

A sheriff arrived on the scene first. Opening the door of his car to let RaNelle rest while they waited for the ambulance, she spotted her reflection in the side mirror. Burned almost entirely black, her face was bloody and cracked. Her chin, her lips, and her nose were completely burned away. Her head and face were swollen almost out to her shoulders, and her once long hair was no more than frizzled patches on the top and sides of her charred skull. Horrified at what she saw and unable to contain her terror, RaNelle screamed uncontrollably.

The Wallaces were rushed by ambulance to the hospital, given emergency treatment, and then transferred to a regional burn facility. As the ambulance carried them both to the burn center, RaNelle found herself suddenly free of pain: RaNelle died.

What followed, as she explained it, was an out-of-body experience. Departing from her physical body, RaNelle observed the scene within the ambulance from above, watching as the nurses and technicians tended to her body, which lay on a gurney. Looking down at herself, she viewed her body perfectly intact: no burns, no wounds, no bleeding. But the physical body wasn't all that came into view. She reviewed her entire life as well and came to understand the reasons why she led her life as she had. This was followed by a sense of transparency, one that brought with it a warm welcome of happiness and joy. Then came the slow departure from the welcoming embrace of the love and peace of angelic forces, and even though she resisted, RaNelle regained consciousness. Her life on earth and her mission there, she was told, was not as yet complete.

Now revived, the "journey" that followed was just as astonishing. RaNelle awakened to an onslaught of agonizing pain and discovered she was hooked up to a life-support system. And then, when her body had successfully rallied for life and she no longer needed the life-support system, she began what proved to be the most excruciating pain yet: intensive physical therapy and, over the next months, more than twenty skin-grafting surgeries. Many times she faced these alone. Her husband was able to leave the burn facility after three weeks and returned home to care for their two young children.

Her health fragile, her body constantly raw and sore from surgery, and her extensive internal injuries still healing, physical pain would be her constant companion for a long time. But the physical pain was to have a cohort—emotional strain came along for the ride.

This form of agony would be trying, too. Finally released from the hospital, there was the challenge of adjusting to life *now*. Her body badly scarred, RaNelle had to deal with the reaction of others to the monstrous telltale signs of her accident. One of the most difficult incidents was the heartbreak and humiliation she felt as her children watched her get hand-cuffed and nearly arrested when a restaurant manager saw her in the Jobst mask (to help her grafts and burns heal) and thought RaNelle was there to rob the restaurant. Time and time again, she witnessed the discomfort and shock others felt when they saw her disfigurement. Once she was asked to leave a clothing store in a mall where she had shopped for years, because "her appearance was upsetting customers." But none of the experiences wrenched her heart more than the distress and embarrassment these looks caused her children—especially when those looks were given by their friends and teachers.

And yet, of all these experiences, the most profound was still to come. Pain, anguish, and trying times would produce a victory of spirit, one that provided more than the assurance of being able to cope with being both the object of people's fright and the soother of their fears. The fire that burned her physical-self gave birth to a resilient spirit-self, one that directed her to place the care of her soul first and foremost— before concerning herself with others and before all other activities and responsibilities.

Now centered on correct principles—focused on listening to her heart and the spirit that lay within—another metamor-phosis took shape. Her intention to value and feed her spirit-self made for an admirable person, one her husband revered. With empathy for what they each had endured, and now with a renewed interest in each other, the couple decided their mar-riage was stronger than their differences. They renewed their commitment to each other. Commitment was the key to recre-ating their love, and from it, two more children—a daughter and son—were born.

Children weren't the only sign of new life. A seemingly bot-tomless wellspring of courage arose within RaNelle, evidenced one predawn morning. As she and her husband were preparing to drive to the burn facility where RaNelle was to undergo yet another skin-graft surgery, they spotted a home in their neighborhood on fire. Alarmed for the safety of the people inside, RaNelle ran to the home to offer help. When no one responded to her pounding on the doors, she literally kicked in a door to get into the burning house. Face-to-face with a fire—understandably the greatest of her fears—RaNelle bravely raced through the smoke and flame-filled house, leading a mother and her two children out to safety. It was an incredible feat for even a trained fireman equipped for such a rescue, but it was even more remarkable for RaNelle, a woman from whom a previous fire had stolen so much. She had revisited the most terrifying experience of her life and won over it.

RaNelle did more than conquer her fear of fire that day; she also earned outward admiration and acceptance for her heroic act. Her town christened her birthday "RaNelle Wallace Day," and, citing her for bravery, the mayor awarded her the Mayor's Eagle Award for Heroism. She was named California Woman-of-the-Year and received a letter of recognition from the President of the United States!

Thankful for having survived her tragedy and filled with a sense of gratitude and humility from the outpouring of love—and now being the recipient of numerous awards, citations, and commendations—propelled her into the public's eye once again. Today, RaNelle Wallace uses her celebrity to take her message of compassion and endurance—spiritual, emotional, and physical—to thousands of burn victims and their families, as well as others who might benefit from her counsel and compassion. Her experience became her work, offered up in service to others.

If RaNelle had wanted my daughter to feel "loved and supported," she had succeeded. That's precisely what came about. As she had requested, I gave her book, *The Burning Within*, to "my sister"—my daughter—who promptly put it in her bookcase, thinking it no more than one more book signed by its author (nothing new to a young person who grew up with an author for a mother). Until one day, years later, when she was going through a tough moment in her life. It was then that my daughter came across the book again and, from it, found support from a "sister," one who wanted her to know that she was "courageous and loved."

Reflecting on RaNelle's book and helped by its message, my daughter called me and said, "Mom, sometimes when you're down and feeling like your obstacles are insurmountable, and then you see the courage and strength of someone like RaNelle, you realize that people are more durable than we imagine—that maybe our problems are more minuscule than we think. Reading her book gave me such a sense of calm, a real 'you can do it' courage. I cried knowing how much she had gone through, but at the same time, I felt like she was holding my heart, encouraging me not to place such a big emphasis on the troubles I had. She makes this beautiful and searing statement, listen to this," and my daughter read me RaNelle's words, " 'I had just enough of me torn away on the outside that I was forced to search deeper inside my own soul. And it is there that you will find the answers to life challenges—within.' "

Jennifer was silent for a moment, perhaps once again digesting the author's words, and then remarked, "Isn't that awesome?" Then, without giving me time to agree, she explained, "Her words make me realize the 'fire' that I'm going through is only 'without.' I need to put less emphasis on my problems and instead feed my heart and spirit." Again there was a thoughtful silence and then Jennifer added, "Oh, and Mom, she signed her book 'your sister.' Isn't that beautiful? What a heart-warmer! And though I don't know her, she sure feels like a sister to me!"

RaNelle Wallace. She is so much more than the sum of her commanding presence. Surviving her tragedy led to a spiritual awakening, one that spawned a new clarity of life purpose. Perhaps a part of that purpose is that we might "see" what perfection is all about through her and understand and appreciate more fully that some pearls—especially those of awesome, solitary beauty—take much time and shaping to come about.

Restoring Lost Years

"To live remains an art which everyone must learn, and which no one can teach."

—HAVELOCK ELLIS

I watched as my friend, Karen, looked squarely into her father's eyes. Ever so slowly, her serious expression gave way to a tender smile and then to tears of hard-won gratitude. Lovingly, she placed her hand on his arm so he could walk her down the aisle. She was a beautiful bride, albeit not a blushing, girlish one. It was a vibrant, mature woman of forty-three who walked beside her father—dashing in his double-breasted rental tux perfectly tailored to his portly frame—his face alight with paternal joy. Karen and her husband, Ron, were renewing their vows in a formal ceremony, on this their twentieth wedding anniversary. Befittingly, a beam of sunlight from the stained-glass window washed over Karen's face, illuminating her radiance within.

This day meant more to her than the sixty or so group of family and friends gathered here in Karen and Ron's honor could have imagined. Looking at her proud sixty-five-year-old father, his head held high and chest thrust forward, each of his sparse gray hairs slicked meticulously back in place, I knew it meant equally as much to him.

One of my dear friends and a confidant for many years, Karen and I have shared our stories of victory and sorrow with each other. Within our relationship we've created a safe haven to "let our hair down," a place that is safe to boast and safe to cry. Looking at her now, walking down the aisle in the expensive one-of-a-kind gown of white satin with literally hundreds of hand-sewn beads—a dress she selected and purchased with all the giddiness of a first-time bride—I knew the *real* price she paid for her joy on this momentous family occasion was that of considerable suffering.

The renewal of her vows was *more* than the love story of Karen and her husband. It was also a victory celebration of a healing heart, an occasion that went a long way towards obliterating some of the "old pain" and "unfinished business" that both daughter and father had been harboring. Distanced from one another since her childhood, their return to each other began with a letter, "the letter," as she calls it, and culminated in her father's presence at her side on this joyous day of "getting hitched all over again."

Writing the letter had made her so upset that she found herself in conflict over whether or not she should send it. Her turmoil was so great that she faxed me a copy of the letter and called to ask if we might set aside an evening to talk about it over dinner.

The anguish she felt towards her father was readily apparent in the tone of her letter. "Dear Daddy," the letter began affectionately, only to change its tone immediately, "I don't know why I'm writing this to you. I don't even know *where* exactly to mail it to!" It had been twenty-seven years since she'd even seen or heard from her father. Though Karen considered the futility of writing the letter, her pen was less hesitant—and more honest. "Thinking of you," it scrawled, "reminds me of the hole that growing up in a home without you left in my heart."

Even after so many years, Karen felt the ache of her father's absence in her life. She had evicted him from her mind long ago—yet her heart had filed a missing persons' report in its effort to locate him. "Why should I care where you are?" she demanded. "And why do I still address you as 'Daddy'?" The bittersweet truth was, she was never allowed to be Daddy's little girl.

Though the wave of emotional upheaval must have been draining, Karen was a woman who preferred insolence to melancholy. "You are just a terrible father!" she blurted out loud—and then wrote the words, as well. Her wrath spurred her on. Picking up her pen again, she unleashed the torment. "You weren't there much to take me up onto your lap and wrap your arms around me," she accused, then informed him, "You were the *only* father who didn't show up at my elementary school on the day they announced the winner of the science fair contest." As if transported back in time to her elementary school classroom, the memories of that day came rushing back in all their vivid detail. Karen could see herself and her mother from a distance, a forlorn frown creasing her mother's brow as she wrapped a soothing arm around the shoulders of her daughter. Karen, a slender little girl whose fretting hazel eyes strayed repeatedly towards the door, stood sadly slouching as she watched for her father's arrival. "First place, honey!" her mother congratulated. "Your father will be so proud. He probably had something important to do or he would have been here by now."

They both knew the truth: He was in a bar somewhere.

Shaking her head at the scene, Karen felt a humorless smile tug at her mouth, as her pen returned to the paper to list, "Nor were you there to support me in running for office of the student body in Junior High—which I did because I thought I'd be a hero with you if I won." Recollections of the worker-bee she had been as a child produced a wave of benevolent feelings for that busy little girl. So diligent were her efforts for her father's attention, she'd overachieved for most of her life in an attempt to make him proud of her. Yet, in spite of all her achievements, she'd never met with success in attaining the approval she yearned for most. "Nor were you there to tell me how special I looked in my prom dress—the one that Mom stayed up half the night sewing for me," she wrote. Unspilled tears so clouded her eyes that she could no longer see the very words causing her such deep sorrow, and so she tucked the letter in her desk drawer and stopped writing for nearly two days.

When she felt ready to battle her case against him again, she took the letter out and began writing again. Now she filed all the indictments against him and charged him guilty of the times he spent with his mistress—liquor. "You allowed your drinking to take you away from me and I hated you for it. Hated you and missed you. I could never understand why you wouldn't just quit. Living with a parent who is an alcoholic is worse than having a parent who is dead." Every bit of anger roiling to the surface, furiously she levied judgment. "If you had just died, that would have been easier." Expressing such terrible words scared her, and she laid down her pen—this time for nearly a week.

When she did continue on with her letter, she reread the words she had written. Finding them a true expression of her feelings, they triggered thoughts of other experiences her father had missed out on. "You weren't there to see me proudly march as honorary guide in my Officer Candidate School graduation parade or to pin my second lieutenant bars on me when I finally earned the right to be called an officer in the Marines." Her feelings reaching a rapid boil, she found herself enraged all over again. "Worst of all, you weren't even there to take my arm on the day of my wedding and proudly escort me down the aisle to my awaiting bridegroom!" Karen had found his absence so unforgivable that from the day of her marriage forward, she divorced herself from her father entirely.

Not that this approach dimmed his presence from her mind. With the birth of her only son, Reed, and with her son's every passing birthday, Karen felt the ache of her father's absence—and missed him more than ever. Eventually she decided that her father should be forced to confront all the neglect. Not there for his own grandson! He should be ashamed. So she wrote, "And you weren't there for Reed's birth—nor for his christening, nor his graduation. . . . " Realizing the list of the crimes her father had committed against her could go on forever, she ended the letter with a simple accusation "You weren't there, you weren't there—you just *weren't*!"

"K" was how she signed off. Not "Karen," not "Love, K." Just "K."

"Until I wrote the letter," she told me, "I didn't know how resentful I was. It honestly surprised me. After all, so many years have passed. Quite frankly, I didn't realize I still harbored so much malice, nor that the pool of pain was so immense."

I assured her it takes time to work out feelings like these. She was less sympathetic. "I'm angry," she railed. "I'm angry because he's an alcoholic and because he shared so little of his time with me in childhood. He made me feel I was worth so little to him. And I'm angry because he caused more bad times than good times for my mother. And because he cheated me out of a father and my son out of a grandfather—and even cheated Ron out of a father-in-law." Finally pausing, she asked in a quieter voice, "Is my anger justified or am I trumping up the charges?"

"I'm sure part of your anger is from not getting the love you wanted and needed," I answered and then counseled, "and magnified by the love you needed to give to him but couldn't because he wasn't around."

"So do you think he'll respond to my letter? Or do you think it will only make him stay away longer?" she asked point-blank.

"I think your letter lets him know how angry you are. But it's been my experience that anger mostly keeps others at bay. Even so, if he doesn't respond—or doesn't respond in the way you want him to—at least you've gotten your feelings out and let him know exactly what they are." My words didn't offer much consolation.

Her anger spent, with tears in her eyes and in a soft voice void of anything other than love and longing, she confessed, "I'd love to have my father back. I'd give anything to have him love me—and his grandson and all of us who want and need his love. Why won't he *need* us?" Her heart ached and I felt for her pain. But an aching heart can be a pain that gets our attention, the first step to sorting things out. In Karen's case, she was both tired of pining for her father and worn out from the torment that missing him caused.

Karen couldn't know that her father had stopped drinking and had been sober some two years prior to receiving her letter. And, for six months prior to her letter's arrival, he had been asking around for advice on what approach might prove most successful in reuniting him with his daughter. He knew she was angry with him, and justifiably so. Should he just show up on her doorstep one day and ask her to forgive him? Should he simply wait until she wanted to contact him? Should he contact relatives or a friend of hers to see "where she stood"? Though he wanted to make amends to his only child, he just didn't know where or how to begin.

And then one day, her letter arrived. The father greeted "the letter" with so many tears that it took him nearly an hour to read it thoroughly. And then he read it and read it again, day after day, for three days. Then he sent her a letter of his own, one he had written so long ago—and rewritten and rewritten, as he searched for the words that might open the door to her forgiveness. His letter to her arrived just six days after she had mailed her letter to him.

She was amazed and surprised.

And didn't know what to do next.

So she didn't reply to his letter.

Not receiving anything from her in return didn't stop the father from writing his daughter. As though a floodgate had been opened, he wrote and wrote, pouring out apologies and offering explanations for some of the things he realized his daughter didn't know, but needed to—such as that day he hadn't come to her elementary school. He had been pulled over for speeding that day, he explained, and was taken to jail on outstanding warrants. He blamed himself, taking responsibility for what he himself had caused, but he wanted his daughter—a daughter he loved dearly even if he hadn't shown it then—to be apprised that, contrary to what she believed, he hadn't forgotten her science fair contest. In fact, it was very important to him that he be there with her that day—it was just, as he explained it, "my actions caught up with me."

Karen read these letters—and reread them—with mixed emotions, but did nothing. It was his fifth letter that touched her heart and caused her to lay down the shield she had been using to guard herself from the pain of her anger towards him. Closing his heartfelt letter by quoting from the Old Testament (Joel 2:25), he wrote, "I will restore to you the years that the locust hath eaten . . . and the cankerworm, and caterpillar and the palmerworm," and then pleaded, "I'd like for us to restore the lost years, Karen. I need my daughter, my 'little girl.' I have missed you so much and cheated us out of so much. Please say that you will let me make it up to you. Please. Love, Dad."

Over the next year, Karen and her father cautiously began a slow dance of getting to know each other. They talked about painful times. Whenever these memories loomed too great or hurt too much, each would back away for a brief period of time. Sometimes this was for a couple of weeks, sometimes for a couple of months. And when the list of hurts between them seemed to be exhausted, they began to do more than rehash the lost years. They began to live in the present. They talked about their relatives, comparing notes about where each family was living and things each was doing. Next, father and daughter began looking forward, disclosing to each other upcoming plans and goals and desires for the coming months. This brought the relationship to a new phase. Suggesting that they do more than converse through letters and phone calls, they began to make room in their lives for one another. Karen flew to Ohio and stayed in a hotel for a weekend to visit with her father. Four months later, she and Ron flew her father to Denver, where they lived, to spend the upcoming Christmas holidays. That was a big step and a happy one.

Six months later brought yet another significant break-through: Her father gave up his apartment in Ohio and moved to Denver, relocating within a few miles of his daughter and her family. This afforded even greater opportunities for them to *do* things together, experiences that began to create a store-house of positive memories. These happy and affirming times fueled an even greater desire to remove old hurts.

It was a lot of work. Tough work. More than Karen realized.

At first there was a lot of "moaning" as she calls it, now looking back, and then a good deal of time spent on "repair." After considerable time rehashing these things, they made a mutual decision to let these things "belong to the *past.*"

Healing would span an even greater amount of time than the time spent on these together. But both father and daughter were committed to gaining each other's love and respect. In time, each would ask the other to forgive all past transgressions.

Now, attending my friend's twentieth wedding celebration, it was apparent how far father and daughter had come.

A week after her twentieth anniversary, Karen and I met for lunch. "I have something I want you to read," she said holding up a letter, a look of pure delight on her face. "I wrote this to my father. You've been with me through our reunion and you know me so well. I want you to tell me what you think."

"Why a letter?" I asked. "Why not tell him in person?"

"I want him to have a letter," she responded. "A record of how I feel. Goodness knows he has ample of those where I spilled out my accusations—though I do believe he has tossed them all out, at least he implied he did. Read it and tell me if it sounds all right." Remembering that the last time she had asked me to approve a letter—one she already had sent, I asked, "Is this one you're considering sending or one that has already been mailed?"

"Just give me your opinion," she said laughing and ignoring my question.

"Dear Daddy, I want to tell you how much walking down the aisle on your arm meant to me. It must have meant a lot to you, too—seeing how you slept in your tux that night—as if taking it off would somehow break the magic spell that was binding us together! I know you have a wisdom born of hard-earned experience and a reverence for life that comes from nearly destroying it. I'm proud of you for taking charge of your life and getting sober instead of sinking into an untimely death. I can see how diligently and lovingly you have worked for your recovery—and the new friendship we now have. I am so very happy that we now have a chance to 'get back' the years we lost. Thank you for the time you now spend with me—the talks, the phone calls—and those priceless letters you've written me which contain the fatherly advice you give me, even if twenty-plus years late! I just might need more of that advice in years to come. After all, you are my Daddy. I guess all daughters want to be Daddy's little girl, even long after they've grown up. Thank you for loving me enough to come back to me. And for all the hard work that made it so. I love you very, very much. Your daughter, Karen."

"It's beautiful," I said, validating my friend's need to see if I approved of the "new place" she was in with her father. "You must share it with him."

"I know," she said. "I mailed it to him this morning!"

Pain—such as that caused from a broken relationship with ones we love—is an irritant from which a pearl can be created. If we are willing to lay down the shield we use to protect ourselves from the pain of not getting—or giving—the love we need; if we are willing to work through the troubled times; if we allow our vulnerable hearts to be exposed to the salve of forgiveness; then we can heal the wounds that bind us—just as Karen and her father did—and recreate love and trust.

Such pearls—*because* they are so hard won—are cherished all the more.

Forty-Four
Gladiolas

"The fragrance always remains in the hand that gives the rose."

—HEDA BÊJAR

"What are you doing, Mommy?" my little five-year-old daughter asked while I was digging holes for fifty gladiola bulbs.

"Planting gladiolas, honey," I answered. "They're my favorite flower."

"More than anything else?" she asked in wide-eyed innocence.

"More than anything else, honey," I replied.

"I wish I had given them to you," she lamented and then sat down and cried. And cried. "*I* want to give them to you," she sobbed, heartbroken at having lost the opportunity to give me something I valued so much.

"Well, then," I remarked, playing into her need to show me her love, "whichever ones you hand me, I will believe with all my heart they are from you!" There remained only six bulbs to plant.

The next week it was Mother's Day. To my surprise my little daughter presented me with a gift, a white shoe box on which she had drawn blooming flowers. Unable to contain her anticipation of my response to her gift, she put her small hands to her glee-filled face and squealed in delight, "Now you can say ALL of them are from me!"

The box was filled with gladiola bulbs — forty-four of them! My daughter had dug up the bulbs I had planted the week prior so that when I [re]planted them, they would be from her.

It's been said that *getting* love is a human requirement. Perhaps *giving* love is a need as well. Certainly this was true of my young child that day. The bulbs, clumps of dirt and all, were her way to express her love and desire to give, to provide a gift she knew I'd find pleasing. Her earlier heartache at losing out on a chance to give resulted in her unearthing a solution, which was to show her love by giving.

The simple act of giving love is the most priceless pearl of all.

Passion
in the
Park

"Nobody sees a flower, really—it is so small we haven't time, and to see takes time."
—GEORGIA O'KEEFE

Patricia wanted the things she wanted. Money, power, prestige, independence, and control topped the list. She believed the surest route to acquire these was to become an attorney—so that was her goal. An olive-skinned beauty with long dark hair and large dark eyes that shined with professional purpose, she was armed with abundant intelligence—or in the words of her law professor, "Patricia Stone has a mind like a steel trap." This serious, no-nonsense, ambitious, dressed-for-success, in-your-face girl was out to achieve her dreams.

No one doubted that she would.

Just twenty-two and already in her final year of law school, Patricia ranked third in a class of 340 students and was well on her way to attaining her goal.

Even her motto revealed her will to win: "Dazzle 'em with brilliance!" In her first year of law school a professor had asked each student to write a mission statement. Hers had been: "Destined for the Supreme Court."

If destiny had plans for seating her on the Supreme Court, it would be from a wheelchair.

Waking up in the hospital, Patricia felt disoriented by the pain in some parts of her body and strangely disassociated from other parts. Then the car accident came back to her, a collage of sensory images flashing through her mind: the bright sunlight of a summer Houston morning being eclipsed by the sight of her friend who was behind the wheel having a seizure, the feel of the car careening out of control, the rusty taste of adrenaline, the sounds of screeching brakes and tires, of breaking glass, and crunching metal. Then darkness.

Though ten calendar days had passed, Patricia's time clock had virtually come to a stop as she'd constantly drifted in and out of consciousness. She had also survived ten hours of major surgery. Though her senses were fuzzy from the medications, Patricia heard the muzzled voices of people in the room. Straining to make out the images, she saw two men standing at the foot of her bed—one was obviously a doctor and the other was a young man holding a bouquet of roses. Through the cobwebs of semiconsciousness she realized the man holding the roses was her boyfriend, Brian. Then she heard the doctor's words: "A broken arm, a broken leg, a broken back . . . " Though she couldn't make out the next couple of phrases, even her fogged state couldn't drown out the words "paralyzed—permanently."

As though keeping these words at bay could prevent them from being admitted as evidence, evidence that meant she would have to rethink her case—the case for her entire life—

she squeezed her eyes shut. But closing her eyes only seemed to amplify the power of the words, so they hurt her even more. In her mind, she saw herself sitting in the courtroom in chains, like a sentenced criminal. "No. No. Wrong role," she told herself. "I'm the attorney!" But as suddenly as the thought occurred to her, her trial was over. "I sentence you to be paralyzed for the rest of your life," the judge ordered. "From now on, you will serve your life in a wheelchair!" His gavel fell with a thud, as he announced, "Case closed."

Serve her life imprisoned in a wheelchair? Patricia couldn't fathom ever accepting such a ruling—certainly not without a fight. "Wait, Your Honor!" Patricia screamed, "I object! You haven't even heard my closing arguments!" It was no use. A bailiff stepped behind her, grabbing the back of her wheelchair and pushing her from the courtroom. Her sentence had begun.

Now in a darkened jail cell in her mind, even in her semi-coherent state, Patricia suddenly realized that the two men in her hospital room were leaving. "Hey, you can't just leave like this!" she shouted. "Tell me, damn it! I demand that you tell me what happened."

The doctor looked at Patricia, seeming to weigh his response. "You've been in a car accident," he gently informed her, his compassionate eyes intently watching her reaction. "You have a few broken bones, but you'll be okay. These things take time. You'll have to be patient. . . . "

Patience was not among her virtues. "Don't patronize me," she accused. "I want to know! I have a *right* to know!"

"In time," the doctor said calmly. Then, turning to summon the nurse, he instructed, "She'll need a sedative." Patricia's attention frantically spun to the other man, and she was startled to find that her boyfriend was no longer in the room. He had set the flowers on a hospital tray and slipped out quietly, too uncertain what to say to her after learning of her "condition."

"Where's Brian?" she asked urgently.

"He left a note . . . ," the nurse began.

"Read it to me," Patricia ordered. Picking up the note, the nurse complied, reading aloud, "Was here to say 'Hi.' Get well. I'll call later."

He never did.

Several weeks passed and Patricia still couldn't quash the memory of the courtroom scene she'd visualized when she learned she was paralyzed from the waist down. Like the video clips of her presiding over mock trials in her law school classes, Patricia replayed her mind-video again and again. In slow motion, the disturbing facts replayed, always remaining the same.

But not nearly as disturbing as the fact of her real life. Her legs were paralyzed—permanently. There was no changing that. Permanently meant forever.

There were people who, like her boyfriend, left her life permanently, as well. The friend who had been driving the car at the time of the accident was one of them. She sustained some injuries, a broken pelvic bone, some bruises. Yet, she walked out of the hospital. Patricia could only hope to roll out in a wheelchair. Perhaps it was guilt that kept her away, or perhaps, like others, she didn't know what to say or do in the face of Patricia's permanent disability. "So young . . . so much promise . . . what a pity," some of her friends murmured.

Family members and other friends remained steadfast, offering condolences and words of encouragement. The trained professionals who surrounded her at the hospital also offered their assurances. Patricia was anything but gracious in accepting them. "Handi-cap-able!" she scoffed when the term was first spoken to her by the hospital's staff psychiatrist. "I'll be a damned handicap for the rest of my life. My life is over—ruined! I can't even walk out of this hospital on my own two legs. Tell me someone is going to hire an attorney in a wheelchair."

"There is no reason you can't complete your degree and continue with your plans to be an attorney. You've lost the use of your legs, not your brilliant mind," the staff psychiatrist countered.

"Easy enough for you to say, you've got your practice and you're still walking on your own legs! And you've already got a husband and had your kids. How do you expect me to pretend I'll be just fine without that?" Patricia grilled with disdain. "C'mon, tell me my boyfriend is going to propose marriage—or even call or visit me again." That silenced her.

"You'll find a way," family and friends continually assured her. Yet as the leaves on the trees outside slowly turned into a collage of gold and orange tinged with crimson, still she remained angry and bitter, and steadfastly rejected anyone's words of encouragement. And when the blend of chestnut and scarlet leaves had long drifted from the trees, leaving barren trunks to stand like gnarled sentinels guarding the outside of her hospital window, still, she remained locked inside her prison, refusing anyone's help or encouragement to move on to the next phase of her life.

One very cold day she moved out of the hospital and into a rehabilitation facility where her assigned goal was to learn how to live her daily life from a wheelchair. And that's about what it was: assigned. She refused to learn even the most basic of skills, such as how to get herself in and out of her wheelchair without assistance, a task she still hadn't succeeded in conquering on her own.

Returning to her room after a session with the physical therapist one day, Patricia was tired and particularly irritable. "Someone named Amy stopped by to see you," Anna, her nurse, informed her cheerfully.

"Great! Where is she?" Patricia asked, a little spark of excitement flickering to life at the thought of a visit from Amy, who had been her friend since junior high school. Brushing back her bangs, she ran her hand through her hair, which she'd haphazardly clipped back in a ponytail, eagerly awaiting Anna's reply.

"I don't know. She came about an hour ago," Anna answered.

"Did you tell her where I was?"

"I told her you were in physical therapy."

"Well, did you tell her how to get there?" Patricia interrogated.

"Well, no."

"I cannot believe you cannot direct a visitor to a physical therapy room!" Patricia snapped. Then snapped. The simple statement had been the thread that broke the camel's back. Launching into an awful tirade, she detailed everything she found intolerable. When finally she could think of no more, she spun her chair around and forcibly wheeled herself out of the room, over to the elevator, and then rode it down to the first floor! Scowling with frustration and squinting with determination, Patricia wheeled herself out of the hospital and into the parking lot. She'd had it with these incompetent people, with this whole nightmare! Each powerful thrust of her good arm was fueled with enough anger to keep her chair at a clip that matched her huff. But then, exhausted and only halfway across the parking lot, Patricia stopped and looked around—and realized there was nowhere for her to go! And besides, she needed her catheter changed—something she hadn't as yet wanted to learn to do on her own.

Grudgingly, she slowly returned to her room.

The nurse was there—waiting for her. Nonetheless, Patricia wasn't about to let Anna help her. She still had some anger-energy left, and she intended to use it! Wheeling to her bed, she forcibly maneuvered herself out of her chair and into the bed—all by herself.

Anna just smiled.

Noting the nurse beaming, Patricia barked, "What? What are you looking at?"

The nurse said simply, "Someone who just got out of her chair—alone."

As the importance of Anna's words struck her, Patricia's haughtiness dissolved and the young woman couldn't help but laugh at herself. It was an awakening, a breakthrough. She had overcome her first hurdle. She *could* do something on her own. She was "handi-cap-able."

This new perspective was helpful.

As this bright young woman came to see herself as more capable, she softened. One of the first noticeable signs was that she became more playful. The many stuffed animals she received from friends, family, and well-wishers—previously stashed away in the closet and stacked on the chairs in her room—now hung from the frame of her bed. Walking down the rehab halls, people would notice the abundance of stuffed toys and stop to comment on them. Some of the other patients made a point of passing by her door to get a look at them or steered others to her room so that they could take in the sight of the plethora of colorful and spirited-looking toys. This lead to a discovery that amazed Patricia: She wasn't the only one who needed uplifting; others needed to be shown encouragement, thoughtfulness, and friendliness. They, too, needed a reprieve from their frustrations, feelings of inadequacy, or setbacks caused by the accidents or illnesses that had befallen them.

Having discovered the toys brought such delight, Patricia now intentionally arranged them to face the hallway where they could readily be seen through her open door—as though they were, first and foremost, for the benefit of others. What came back to her was their genuine appreciation and a friendliness she had never imagined—especially given to someone they didn't even know. A kind word and a courteous gesture had been so simple and yet had done so much. This led to the discovery that she had a greater need to interact with others than she would have ever suspected. She realized that she had cut herself off from others far too long. She found a remedy for this too.

As she grew to appreciate the kindness and courtesy people showed to her, she began to offer it back. She asked her brother to bring her guitar to the hospital and began to play it for others. She knew music lifted her spirits; now she took pleasure in the fact that it lifted the spirits of others as well. People began to seek her out, to ask her to play her guitar for them. This pleased her and made her feel desired and needed. More aware of how much people meant to her, she enjoyed the smiles and pleasure she brought them. Reflecting on just how fast she'd been traveling through her life, she realized just how much she had missed as a result. Once a "type A," Patricia rarely had time for idle conversation. But what she once thought of as "idle chatter" no longer seemed unimportant. Now she saw those who stopped to talk to her as her window to the world.

Interacting with others offered new information and perspective on how she might transform her life. As she listened to their experiences and learned how they were planning to move forward with their lives—some of them recovering from injuries far worse than her own—she gained hope for her life beyond the rehab center and began to focus on joining the "real world" once again. Their enthusiasm spawned her own.

As expected, there have been *many* changes in Patricia's life. The woman we encounter radiates a certain peace and contentment. She's very patient, a good listener, an optimist. She has a vibrant personality and a very definite energy and spunk about her. When I ask her about what she does for fun and excitement, she smiles broadly and answers, "Well, staying fit is always an issue for me and I've always loved to travel. I always thought of travel as something I'd do after I'd become successful and had made some money, but I've found a source to travel and stay fit at the same time. I've been a member of the United States Women's Wheelchair Basketball Team for five years, and this year I've been to Venezuela and England! We won the gold in Venezuela and the bronze in England."

"That's ambitious!" I remark, to which she says, "I don't think of it as ambitious as much as fun and a great workout— and a great way to meet people." Laughing, she admits, "I was never that great an athlete before the accident. It took a wheelchair to make me work hard enough to be good! Then, I have my friends," she says and with a special sparkle in her eyes, "and John."

"A boyfriend?" I ask.

"Maybe," she says, smiling slyly and then adds, "I'm so people oriented now. It's a new dimension, and one I really like. I feel like I belong to the human race. It's absolutely amazing how people go out of their way to hold a door for me so that I can get through it easier. They take the time to talk to me. It's a very special way to live." With a look of satisfaction on her face, she remarks, "I'm okay. I have a sense of being needed. I travel, I have love in my life, and I have my work. It's what everyone needs, what everyone would like to have. I don't feel sorry for myself anymore." With a hardy laugh she declares, "I don't have time for that!"

Being sensitive, I venture cautiously. "I find it remarkable—and notable—that you have such a gracious edge of gratitude as it relates to the accident."

"I don't have the perception of what happened to me as a *tragedy*," she explains, casually tossing her long, lustrous curls over her shoulder, "just a major inconvenience." Smiling, her beautiful, large, dark eyes seasoned with empathy, compassion, and a maturity gained not with years but from having gone through such a harrowing, life-altering ordeal, she adds, "I've heard it said that 'when one door is closed, another one opens.' For me, being in a wheelchair opened the door to a world I'm convinced I would have never discovered if I hadn't slowed down enough to see the beauty in life. I've discovered a love for painting that is even greater than the desire I had for becoming an attorney. It's a passion I'm so excited about that I work well into the night and, still, I can't wait to get up out of bed each morning and begin again."

"Passion in the park: The underworld of nature at its boldest?" I ask, noting her recent award-winning collection of paintings.

"Yes!" she laughs, her eyes sparkling with levity at her good fortune. "Of all places, I found passion in the park. Wheeling my way through the winding paths of the park one day, everything just seemed particularly vibrant and alive. It wasn't just the brilliant sun or the sky glistening bright blue, it was as if some distant reality had moved closer. From my wheelchair, so many things *were* so much closer. I'd never noticed how vivid and varied the colors of the blades of grass could be. I was eye-level with all kinds of newly blossoming flowers. Awed by their beauty, I was amazed that I could have missed them all those times through the years when I'd jogged through the park.

"There were flowers with three slick, spiraled shoots that had dark green leaves striped with light green, and white and yellow brightly framed with red edges. How could I have overlooked them? Have you ever seen a Mimosa?" she asks rhetorically, her excitement obvious in her animated expression. "They have these little blossoms of violet flowers that look just like tiny cheerleading pom-poms. I was enchanted by them! I studied intricate cones of yellow petals with small white sprays springing randomly from them like geysers of billowy foam. All the different colors and shades, the delicate designs and textures, the blossoms within blossoms—I was overwhelmed. I felt like Dorothy waking up in Oz!

"In the weeks that followed I returned to the park time and time again, drawn there by this mysterious curiosity to explore this small intricate underworld of nature at its boldest. I'd never painted before, but I discovered that recreating the intricacies, the colors, the beauty of the flowers in the park and sharing them is absolutely my life's work. I am just compelled to capture those images. What's amazing is that I also discovered my heart had the ability to capture them all *perfectly*. To bring alive such beauty, to reanimate it in all its splendor on canvas, and to be able to share it with others is such a gift."

Eventually Patricia did go back to college, but it was to study something entirely different than law. Instead, she zealously pursued her passion for painting—a seemingly boundless passion that is complemented by an equal measure of talent. She now shares the beauty of the tiniest intricacies of nature with the legacy of her volumes of paintings, a collection so extensive that she is opening a gallery of her own! And though she isn't talking about it yet, there is also John (or "Dr. John," as she is fond of calling him). An art professor she met at the university, John is a widower with three children, ages five, six, and fifteen. He is also the man to whom Patricia has recently become engaged.

"When one door closes, another door opens." What a generous gift! Sometimes we receive this gift only when one door has been closed to us and we are pushed through another door that has been opened. Understandably, in the wake of the accident, Patricia had to mourn the loss of many things. It took time and hard work. Trials often do. But for Patricia, it was on the wings of her disability that she was granted a special gift, one akin to her deeper nature, a pearl that allows her to fulfill her motto: "Dazzle 'em with brilliance!"

And, of course, she was offered a family. On that, the jury is still out!

Hunting for Wild-Child

"Nothing can match the treasure of common memories, of trials endured together or quarrels and reconciliations and generous emotions."
— ANTOINE DE SAINT-EXUPÉRY

Clarine gently picked up the jewelry box in the department store, admiring its treasure-chest shape and the colorful, inlaid jewel-shaped stained-glass designs on its lid. Reaching out to place it back on the shelf, she happened to glance down at her watch. It was almost two o'clock. *"Oh, I better get going,"* Clarine thought. *"Hayden will soon be getting home from playing bridge."* She smiled serenely at the thought, as she momentarily visualized him sprightly ambling into the house, whistling, his face animated, eyes skipping with an added sparkle. Hayden was always so full of life—and new jokes— after his few hours spent with "the boys."

She and Hayden had been married forty-one years and were, quite simply, the center of each other's lives. It was a good marriage filled with the usual ups and downs of family life, one they had always characterized as fulfilling. They raised three daughters, finally paid off their "dream home" and planned a future designed with the two of them in mind. A winsome smile played on her lips, as Clarine reached up to tenderly finger the gold heart pendant he had given her on their fortieth anniversary. As suddenly as her smile appeared, it fell as she was startled by reality: Her husband *wouldn't* be getting home from his regular Saturday bridge game. Hayden hadn't gone to play bridge at all. He died ten months ago.

Instantly, tears welled up in her eyes. Tears always seemed to nest just below the surface and were all too willing to spill at the mere memory of Hayden. Hayden had been gone ten months, and she *still* lived in sync with the life they'd lived as a couple.

Clarine felt simply lost without him—in more ways than one. Like last Tuesday, when she promised to meet her friend Katherine at a restaurant downtown, a restaurant she had frequented many times with Hayden. As she entered the downtown area where the restaurant was located, Clarine realized she didn't know exactly how to get to it. While she knew it was "over there, in that direction," she was unsure what street to turn onto. She found herself genuinely baffled by the hectic traffic and downright scared when she turned into oncoming cars on a one-way street. *How could she be so dumb?* She'd been downtown with Hayden many times. But she hadn't really paid attention when Hayden had been driving.

It seemed there was no end to the "little" things she had relied on Hayden to do. This was never more clear to her than last month when she'd gone to see their attorney. After leaving his office she walked to the elevator, only to realize she didn't know if she should push the "up" or the "down" button. She had no idea where she had parked the car! Not only had she forgotten to mentally record the aisle and parking space in the parking garage, she hadn't even taken note of the floor! She never forgot to check when she went places she was used to going alone, but she had never driven to the attorney's office without Hayden. When she and Hayden had visited their attorney, knowing where the car was parked had been his responsibility. Clarine had grown so used to Hayden driving, Hayden holding the keys, Hayden keeping track of where the car was parked, she no longer paid attention to relying on herself. *"Can't I do anything alone?"* she asked herself. *"Have I lost myself completely?"* Her idealized self-image carried with her since childhood was of a self-reliant, capable woman. Now, without Hayden, she seemed anything but. Now life was so very complicated. She was overcome with self-doubt, as if her very identity was in question. Yet, she knew she would *have* to go on without him. She just wasn't sure how to do that. Breaking forty-one-year-old habits would take some time. Clarine wasn't prepared to erase their lives together . . . nor their dreams together. The jewelry box still in her grip, she now set it down, wondering when she would stop slipping back in time. Again feeling utterly alone, Clarine bowed her head and stood there in the store and just cried.

A hand gently touched her shoulder and a soft voice asked, "Are you all right?" Clarine looked up to see a young man, perhaps no older than her oldest granddaughter. "What's wrong?" he repeated with genuine concern. Clarine believed he really wanted to know. So she told him how she'd lost her husband ten months before, how she'd turned the wrong way up the one-way street, how she'd forgotten the floor and stall number in the huge parking garage. She told him how she'd even forgotten her daughter's birthday last month, and finally, how she had now found herself in the store thinking she needed to hurry home because she was still living a life that no longer existed.

The young man listened, not really knowing what to say. His stupefied silence made Clarine realize even more clearly that while life without Hayden seemed nearly impossible, she had to let go of a shared life and move forward alone. She couldn't even reply, "I'm just remembering and feeling sad. But thanks for your concern."

"I'll be okay," she finally told the young man, "and thank you for being so kind. I'll be okay . . . *really.*"

"When will this deep sadness go away?" she wondered, as she left the store. Then she remembered a dear friend had told her that one of the first things she did after the death of her husband was to replace their double bed with a single bed. Her husband's empty space in their bed was a constant reminder of his absence and made her sad every time she looked at it, let alone climbed into it. Now painfully aware of what her friend had meant, Clarine knew she had to make changes in her life, too. Her memories of Hayden and their lives together couldn't be taken away nor diminished with time. Finding herself telling her life story to a young stranger of barely twenty, Clarine knew it was time to rebuild a life—a life without Hayden. Now it was up to her to find the car—and the keys, and the restaurant! She had to learn to take care of herself. *"But how?"* she asked herself as she got into her car. *"Just do something!"* she told herself. *"You've got to change!"*

Change began at home.

"Do you think that changing the pictures would make the house feel different?" she asked each of her daughters. "The pictures are just fine, Mom," her girls replied. But Clarine wasn't so certain things were "just fine" as they were. She and Hayden had married when she was nineteen. She had gone from high school to marriage, straight from her parents' house into a home with Hayden. She'd never lived alone. She pondered this fact. Now she did live alone, and she could do whatever she pleased with her house. What was her style anyway? Hayden had preferred blues and plaids. She'd always decorated her home with him and the children in mind. Now she didn't have to consider what anyone else would prefer. Would she like bright colors, or did she prefer more subtle earthtones? Would she like the decor flowery, or frilly, or more simple?

After careful consideration and much time browsing through mail-order catalogs and wandering in and out of stores, Clarine spent months redecorating each room of her home to suit her taste—a whimsical, feminine, Victorian style. She changed nearly all the large wall art and many of the photos sitting around her home. At first her kids worried about her, thinking she was making too many changes too soon. "I'm trying to see it like an adventure rather than frightening," she informed them.

"I'm not sure I like that wall decor, Mom," one of her daughters said.

"You may not like it, but I do," she replied.

"You're not overdoing it, are you?" another asked.

"No, looking for just the right colors, pieces, and knick-knacks was like being on a treasure hunt of sorts."

"But aren't you going a bit overboard, Mom? I mean, it's like a different house."

Delighted, she responded, "Wonderful, that was my goal!"

"But Mom, mauve carpeting throughout? Isn't that a drastic change from the practical person you've always been?"

"I haven't always been practical," she retorted. "But I've *always* loved mauve."

Turning the house into *her* home (and standing her ground with her daughters) gave Clarine the courage to set out on another treasure hunt. This time she would "redecorate" herself. She began by coloring her hair, changing it from gray to a soft brown. She joined the gym and cleaned out her closet. This makeover led to her digging deeper to uncover who she was at this drastically new and unplanned point in her life. It was an introspective phase, one in which she no longer felt as if she were "drowning in the emptiness of time." Now she relished the hours and days she scheduled with no other plans than to be alone with herself. During these times she would carefully prune flowers or slowly weed the garden, activities that allowed her to think deeply about a new and pressing series of questions: *Who am I? Who am I outside of widow or mother, volunteer and community activist? How should I fill my days? What do I want to do? What have I always done but no longer want to do? What have I not done but always longed to do? What makes me happy—most happy?*

Clarine was surprised to discover that while sorting out the answers to these questions, the reoccurring vision in her mind was of herself as the teenager who loved to dance and had gone dancing often. With this image in mind she asked, *"What happened to that capable, free-spirited, wild-child girl in me, the go-getter, the risk-taker?"* Of all the questions, she moved this one to the top of the list.

It was good placement. When a girlfriend from the neighborhood coaxed her into attending a senior's dance, at first hesitant, Clarine recalled that it was Hayden who didn't like to dance—not her. She decided to appease the calling of the free spirit within. It wasn't long before her swing and jitterbug were as lively and well-choreographed as they'd been in her youth. "Mom is having a midlife crisis later than most," her daughters teased. Now in their late thirties, they watched with amusement—and mild disbelief—as their mother "got in touch" with that "wild-child girl" she had traded in so many years ago.

Dancing, just one of the gems in Clarine's new treasure chest, had facets she hadn't even considered. Seniors, she found, often lead very active lives, and there were more socials and outings than she'd ever imagined. There were trips to libraries, plays, movies, and museums; there were volunteer organizations for children's homes, hospitals, "pet-N-plant" sitting. There were socials that included singles dances, all-ladies groups and mixed groups, and there were cruises—two-day cruises to twenty-one-day cruises. She found her new friends and her new life of interesting activities refreshing. And rejuvenating. When two friends asked her to consider going with them on an eight-day cruise, she fondly recalled she and Hayden hadn't gotten around to that.

Now, Clarine did.

Yet, perhaps there was no greater cruise than the one Clarine set sail for within her own heart. Destined for an island paradise of the soul, she sought to retrieve the treasure of the self buried within. It was an adventure of rebuilding a life to suit her interests and talents at this juncture of her life, one that led to the discovery of the often subtle jewels of self. Reclaiming these jewels renewed her sense of girlish wonder, spontaneity, and energy, adding zest, zeal, and joy to her life. Taking steps towards being self-reliant brought with it a heightened sense of self-esteem. She discovered that the more of life she lived, the less of it she feared! And so she discovered a paradox in being social—it also led her to a sense of comfort with being alone.

Heartache had been a diligent messenger, delivering the realization that the independent, fun-loving, and capable girl could coexist hand-in-glove with the loving, memories she and her husband had created together. The human spirit, resilient as ever, had triumphed. Now, there was real truth to the words Clarine had spoken to the young man in the store that day—"I'll be okay . . . *really.*"

Most Wanted

> "On a night when the moon shines as brightly as this, the unspoken thoughts of even the most private heart might be seen."
>
> —IZUMI SHIKIBU

For John Walsh, July 27, 1981, began like many other days. Awake at seven, John read the paper, ate breakfast with his wife and son, and then went off to work. Yet the day was to become one that would forever alter the course of John's life.

July 27, 1981, would painfully loom forever in his mind as the day his only child—a little boy who loved Little League and long walks on the beach with Dad, an adventurous little six-year-old with dark blond hair and an impish smile displaying a budding tooth—disappeared without a trace while he and his mother browsed in a Florida shopping mall. Sick with a fear that only parents whose beloved child has been stolen from them could know, John and his wife, Reve, could scarcely believe it, let alone know what to do about it. Protective by nature, they had taught their son never to wander off or talk with strangers. They didn't let him ride his bike to school, or cross the street, or go to the park by himself. Yet in just five minutes, all their precautions became irrelevant.

They turned away for just one moment and he was gone.

Frantically they searched the entire length of the mall, calling his name and asking everyone, security guards, volunteers, and police, to help in their search. All came up empty handed; there was simply no clue to what had happened to their son.

Two weeks later, after an intensive search and public plea, the dread of the worst became truth. Their little son was dead. Murdered.

The police recovered the little boy's body from a drainage canal.

Racked with the grief of their little boy stolen away from his mommy and daddy, treated so brutally, killed so maliciously, there were simply no words to describe the pain that filled John and Reve Walsh. It was a void they knew could *never, ever* be filled. Feeling helpless, John was overcome with sickness and depression. He couldn't concentrate at work; he couldn't sleep; he lost thirty pounds. Nothing, not even the love and comfort of family and friends, could give him a reprieve from the piercing onslaught of the agony he felt. He contemplated suicide—anything was better than dying from a broken heart.

But anguish was only a part of what he felt. He was also filled with rage. The brutal murder of an innocent child—his child—made absolutely no sense. Driven by his rage and grief, John began a manic search for answers, but discovered there were none. A stranger had taken his son from him—a stranger no one could find. There was not even a suspect in the crime of his little boy's death.

John and Reve decided the only answer to their loss was to fight back, to use the legal system to battle crimes against children, to prevent criminals from striking again, and, ultimately, to bring them to justice. Among the victories of their tireless efforts is the Missing Children Act, the Missing Children's Assistance Act, and the National Center for Missing and Exploited Children, all measures aimed at protecting the rights of parents and children and holding perpetrators responsible and liable for their malicious actions. Yet, for all the great good these provided, the intrusion of pain in their lives produced an even bigger pearl: *America's Most Wanted*, a nationally televised program (created by John Walsh) dedicated to rallying the support of the nation in assisting in the capture of criminals and in seeing them brought to justice. To date, *America's Most Wanted* has been instrumental in putting hundreds of criminals in prison. And, it has brought countless missing children safely home to their families.

We know a deep sense of compassion and sorrow for John and Reve and the unfathomable pain of the loss of their son, Adam. Yet we also know how fortunate we are that from their grief emerged concern and regard for *others*. Due to the tireless efforts and leadership of John and Reve Walsh, victims and their families have support and comfort in their pain—and the support of millions of citizens who rally to their defense and bring a semblance of closure to their injustice by finding and holding criminals accountable for their unjust and horrific acts.

That a child is found, that a criminal is brought to justice, is a testimony to the supreme value of the pain of John and Reve Walsh, and their priceless tribute to the precious life of a little boy they—and we—will never see grow up, but will *always* love nonetheless.

The Most Perfect of Pearls

"Gamble everything for love, if you're a true human being."
—Rumi

Pacing along outside the barbed wire fence in front of the cell her daughter was locked within, day after day, a mother kept vigil. Hour after hour, from the time the sun rose until long after dark, the mother was there. Why this lonely, supreme effort?

When I read of her, my own heart empathized with her anguish and with the love for a child that made it so. Those among us with a mother's heart well know that a child can be a mother's greatest love, but also has the power to inflict her greatest heartbreak. This woman's nineteen-year-old daughter had been incarcerated and stood trial for a crime she had committed. Her daughter was so distraught over what she had done, so filled with remorse and self-hate, that she wanted to take her own life. From the depths of her grief, she told her mother during a visit, "It would be so much easier if I ended my life. I can't accept what I have done! There is no way I can ever forgive myself . . . I can find no reason to go on . . . I don't want to live any longer."

"No!" her mother protested, wanting desperately to reach through the visiting room glass that divided them and hold her daughter close. Her own heart could forgive, and she was unable to fathom even the thought of her daughter taking her own life. "You must choose life," she pleaded. "As hopeless as things seem, you must *not* take your life. No matter what you have done, you are my child. I love you. And *need* you."

"But Mom," the woman-child cried, "I've done this terrible, unthinkable thing; I've been an accomplice to robbing a store—at gunpoint! I threatened an innocent person and realized I *was* capable of pulling the trigger. I can't stop thinking about it, and what a terrible thing I've been a party to. I can't take being alone with my thoughts and I don't have the strength to live in this environment, this cell . . . I feel so alone. I am alone."

Her mother's heart instantly connected and felt for this child of hers. "You are *not* alone," the mother insisted, knowing it was so. Even though her child had done a terrible thing, she would remain faithful to helping her daughter swim through the turbulent waters and reach the shores of better times. She would see her baby learn to walk a righteous path in life, that her child squarely face life's lessons and their consequences, that her now-adult daughter turn her face to the sun and choose hope and life—this was simply her never-ending role as a mother. She would not judge her daughter or reject her. She most especially would not give up hope that her child's soul would win the battle in its fight for light over shadows. She would buoy her daughter somehow. "Promise me that you will not take your life," the nineteen-year-old's mother appealed.

"If only I had your courage and strength," the daughter lamented.

"Then you will," the mother vowed. "Promise me that as long as I am near, you will draw on my courage and strength until you find your own again."

And so each and every day, without fail, the mother came to the prison and stood outside the fence near her daughter's cell. Her daughter could look out her small window and know she was not alone and could thus find the courage to go on, to choose life over death, hope over despair. The mother came at daybreak and stayed until a guard informed her that her daughter was asleep for the night. On many occasions, that wasn't until well after midnight. This the mother did day-in and day-out, week after week, until her daughter had come to terms with her despair and self-loathing and was ready to face the consequences of her actions.

Oh, for the courage and strength of a mother's heart, one ever-willing to come to the aid of its possessor—her child. Perhaps no greater heartstrings can bind one soul to another than those of a mother and child—cords, that if all be told, are stronger than those of other deep ties of love.

As I watched the unfailing loyalty and courage of this mother, I thought of how often my own mother had tirelessly loaned me her support and courage as I paced before the fence of some heartache that imprisoned my own daughter's precious heart. Just last month I called my mother "to talk." This talk quickly opened up to a discussion about a matter that involved my daughter. My mother and daughter have a special relationship that belongs to them alone. When the three of us get together, I instantly recognize their union and feel so grateful for it—as grateful as I feel for the love my mother and I share, one in which we lovingly protect and guard each other's heart. Listening as I poured my troubles out, my mother consoled me, while offering support for a granddaughter who is an absolute soul mate to her. But then, when my mother detected that my heart was heavy and so obviously burdened, her support shifted away from her granddaughter—and even away from her usual rooting for both my daughter and me—and staunchly came to rest on my side alone. This was comforting to me—until I sensed that my mother had strayed a little too far off the side of empathy for my daughter. Then, I began to rally for my daughter and was soon defending her. My mother continued to defend me against my daughter. There was a moment of tension between us, followed by its customary silence, and then simultaneously we both broke into laughter. We each understood what we were doing. We were each defending *our own child!*

My mother loves and adores her granddaughter, so she could be objective—but only until she heard the pining within her own child's heart. Instinctively, she began guarding me against my own child. And I was then defending my daughter against my mother's straying from her defense. It was an insightful moment—and a common one for a mother's heart.

Is this instinct? The work of angels? Or simply a legacy of a heart seasoned by pain, enriched by love, and bound by an innate soul-intelligence? Inextricably tied to her child—and acting from a higher, wiser, more luminous part of herself—a mother willingly ventures into the land so many flippantly call codependence. Armed with a fiercely loyal love and aching protectiveness, a mother's heart tirelessly reaches out to courageously protect and defend her beloved child.

Those who possess a mother's heart can understand why a mother stands by her child—even when a child doesn't always deserve such loyalty. Accepting her all-consuming bond with her child, a mother's heart keeps her vigilance. Day by day. Year after year.

Forever.

It is in the eyes of a mother's heart that we best see a spirit that so often remains undaunted in the face of personal or worldly failures or shortcomings, a courageous spirit that has both unfaltering belief that any heart can thaw the cruelty of its self-destructive ways, and an unwavering faith that "we can get through this." A mother's compassionate spirit is an angel's whisper coaxing us to take the high road, assuring us that doing so is the highest form of humanness.

A mother's heart, quite possibly, is the most perfect pearl of all.

Tortoises Among Us

"There's more to life than increasing its speed."

—GANDHI

He was seven years old at the time—and a guest on *AM Philadelphia*. Smiling with enthusiasm and confidence, the smartly dressed little boy with the large round eyes sparkled as he counted in twelve foreign languages and then used his hands to count perfectly in sign language. What an incredibly delightful and smart kid! Imagine his parents' pride!

But then, since the day he was born—June 27, 1974—Jason Kingsley has always been extraordinary. When he was only fifteen months old, he made his television debut sitting on Buffy Saint-Marie's lap on *Sesame Street* and was a regular on that show until he was sixteen. Not that he settled for just being a star on an award-winning television program attuned to its global audience. In addition to having parts in a number of television movies, including "The Fall Guy"—for which he learned a sixty-four-page script—Jason attended school, remaining on the honor roll throughout. There, the young man with a wondrously curious mind and a playful sense of humor excelled in math (he says he is "mathemagical"!), though he was mostly interested in the study of other cultures—especially Latin America, Southeast Asia, Africa, Afghanistan, Lebanon, Israel, the Middle East, Western and Eastern Europe, China, Japan, and Russia.

Not that academics consumed him. He was also active in Wig 'n' Whiskers, a drama club, and he worked part time. Oh, and while still in high school, he coauthored a book (*Count Us In*) with his best friend, Mitchell Levitz. Their work was so impressive, both boys were invited to appear on *Dateline NBC* to discuss it!

To keep himself fit and full of an unquenchable energy, Jason hikes, swims, likes to fish, and enjoys group sports. He is also a pianist who plays a bit of Mozart and Bach. And he *loves* Broadway musicals! Though inner directed, he's not selfishly self-absorbed. In fact, he's a sensitive young man with a real concern and compassion for others—especially those suffering from war and starvation. And, if you engage him in a conversation about how "planet earth is faring ecologically"—yet another of his favorite topics—you'll learn that he can talk hours on end on this subject, too.

What a multifaceted, interesting, talented, goal-setting, and achieving guy!

In view of the extraordinary scope of Jason's interests and achievements, it's nothing short of disappointing—if not shocking—to learn of the doctor's words just hours after his birth. "Your child is mentally retarded. He'll never sit or stand, walk or talk. He'll never be able to distinguish you, his parents, from other adults. He'll never read or write or have a single meaningful thought or idea. Place him in an institution immediately, and go home and tell your friends and family that he died at birth."

Jason Kingsley has Down syndrome.

At the time their son was born, Jason's mother, Emily, was a writer for *Sesame Street*, a popular national television program created to help young children develop basic skills. Mrs. Kingsley's chief responsibility was to help an audience of children in seven million homes in more than 140 countries learn their letters, numbers, shapes, and the rules for playing fair. What good fortune for Jason: His mother was in the business of helping children learn how to learn! Jason was quickly added to her audience. With all the resolution in the world, Mrs. Kingsley—a mastermind of children's learning—set out to help Jason learn. From sewing quilts of different fabrics, to putting Jason in tubs of flavored Jello to stimulate his learning, Emily Kingsley was bound and determined to help her son develop skills that could help him achieve and succeed in the world, most especially to have a full and happy life.

Not only did Mrs. Kingsley unlock the door to Jason's learning and developing a wide array of social and life skills, she also discovered that finding out *how* Jason learned was useful to her work on the show. If Jason could grasp a concept and retain it, then so could other children. And so Jason's "point of learning" served as the baseline for selecting the methods to teach the children who tuned in to enjoy and learn from *Sesame Street*. Not only did Jason open up new possibilities for the series—*Sesame Street* opened up new possibilities for Jason, as well.

How fortunate for Jason that he was born to parents who refused to allow him to be condemned by the doctor's prognosis, who didn't reject him, and loved him enough to help him have a "full life." Today, as his remarkable achievements attest—with a special thanks to his parents and his pal, *Sesame Street*'s eight-foot, two-inch "Big Bird"—Jason has a full compliment of skills. Moreover, he has an interesting and meaningful life.

How fortuitous that Jason persevered against those dire predictions as well—and proved them all wrong. But we must not think it's been easy for him. Jason struggled arduously to overcome the obstacles inherent in the biological nature of Down syndrome.

Jason's life is a bigger legacy than his lucking out by having parents who helped him become a capable and achieving young man. And it's more than an account of his journey to overcome the obstacles and struggles inherent in being born with special needs. The real value of tallying the ledger of Jason's accomplishments is not just to admire his phenomenal personal achievements, but rather to chronicle the *real worth* behind the words *"each person is special and unique."* Admiring Jason is to look through the lens that brings into view not just that we are special, but that the mark of a successful life is in finding *how* we are special. For Jason, Down syndrome is the vehicle on which he rides into the sunset. Because of it, he has found purpose and direction. It is his *calling.*

The trouper has gladly put on the yoke. Doing what? Doing what the traditional medical establishment suggested he not get a shot at: a chance to live among family and friends, a chance to live a full and happy life. And so he has become a tireless crusader, intensely insistent that others born with

Down syndrome have the chance to make a meaningful contribution to family, school, and community. Jason wants all of us to know that despite their intellectual limitations, children with Down syndrome have a great capacity to give and receive love. He believes that whatever their ultimate level of achievement, they must be allowed to live a full and productive life, to have an opportunity to go down the same road in life as he has.

He couldn't be more suited for his work. Though busy doing many things, none give Jason greater pleasure than talking with parents of children born with Down syndrome. It's his passion, one that has become his avocation. "When parents first learn their baby has Down, they are anxious, a little nervous about this 'different' baby," he tells me. "So I help."

"How do you do that, Jason?" I ask this hard-working, good-natured, good-will ambassador.

"I let them see—in person—what Down syndrome looks like," he tells me, smiling his usual charismatic grin, and then in the same breath adds, "The parents look at me and see how tall I am, how smart I am, and how nice I am and how friendly I am, and when they learn about all the things that I've done, they decide that it's okay for their baby to come home with them. Because of me, they'll be good parents to their baby, and they feel happy and not sad about their baby. That makes me feel proud that I helped them. And I've helped their little baby, too. The little baby will be loved and not left alone or have to live without his parents and brothers and sisters and friends. And now the little baby will get a chance to be taught things and to learn things, because the parents will expect their little baby to be a real person with a normal life. And then, one more little baby will get to have a great life. That's what I *do*! It's my job!" With ever-gleaming eyes, he adds, "What I'm doing is *really* important."

Its importance is evident in his explanation: "When they see me, parents aren't so worried they won't be able to love their baby." Pausing, Jason grows reflective, then adds, "Especially if the doctors have told them things that make them feel the baby will never be able to do anything."

"What are the magical words you use to open them up to all the hopeful possibilities, Jason?" I ask.

"I tell them to not call it 'Down' syndrome but rather 'Up' syndrome, because then they can stay focused on being up and positive," Jason answers. "They have to teach their child to be proud and not ashamed of himself. The parents have to be proud of their child so they will teach him, and their child has to be proud of himself so he can learn and be happy." Soulfully, he adds, "Just because a child has Down syndrome doesn't mean he can't do things. It just takes a little longer."

"So you tell them to be patient," I say.

"Sort of," he replies. "I remind them of the story about the tortoise and the hare. You remember it, right?" he asks, laughing merrily and not waiting for a response. "Being born with Down syndrome means you're the tortoise because you do things more slowly. I'm a tortoise because I have to work much harder at things than other people do, but still, it's not bad to be slow. You learn a lot when you are slow like the tortoise. And you see a lot of things other people don't see, so you really know the scoop on things!" Now dead serious, he leans forward and enunciates each word slowly, "People aren't *losers* just because they're slower than others." Without pausing, Jason lightens up and cheerfully informs, "Don't forget, the tortoise won! Like the tortoise, I'm a winner!—just like all the other people with Down syndrome."

"I'd like to do a story on you, Jason," I say. "May I?"

"Oh, sure," he approves with genuine enthusiasm. "That'd be great!" And then, reflecting on our conversation, he instructs, "Be sure to remind doctors that if you send a baby with Down syndrome to an institution, the baby will miss out on his family's love. And be sure to tell the family that they will miss out on all the love that their baby can give to them. Oh, and one more thing. Tell them the story about the tortoise and the hare. And, don't forget to remind them that the tortoise won!"

Jason Kingsley. A person who entered "the race" and won.

Today Jason Kingsley works tirelessly and enthusiastically for the rights of those with Down syndrome—a condition that affects one in every eight hundred births. Thanks to Jason, parents of children born with Down syndrome have a model—a vision of the possibilities of what their child's life can be. Jason wants us to honor whatever that potential may be. Though some children will never learn to read or write a book, they have no less value and dignity than another child who performs on a higher level. We must celebrate their more modest accomplishments and deem them purposeful.

The commitment of Jason's parents to layer love and teaching upon layer of love and teaching is a powerful example of the pearl that can be formed within a child born with Down syndrome. That Jason finds meaning in helping parents of children with Down syndrome pays tribute to *using* the life you are given, the highest homage we can make to fulfilling our purpose and calling. Jason's life is inspirational because through him we can see more clearly that though we are each unique and special, more than this, we are each *called*. As Jason reminds us, each child must be given a chance to enter the race and to live life to the fullest—even if at the pace of a tortoise.

However long it takes a pearl to become a pearl is quite beside the point: Whether two months or twenty-four months, it was always destined to become a pearl. As Jason reminds us, it helps to remember that "the tortoise won!" Life reminds us!

A "World" According to Eden

"All that matters is what we do for each other."
—LEWIS CARROLL

My good friend, Dianne, asked me to come with her as she helped settle her eighty-three-year-old grandmother into a nursing facility. Walking with "Grandma Mary" between us, the three of us moved slowly down the halls, which were decorated with an eclectic array of frames of all sizes and shapes that held photos of residents and members of their families, the administration and health care staff, cute pets, and an assortment of plants in bloom. As I took in the sight of this interesting and completely un-hospital-like motif, we continued towards a room that would be Grandma Mary's new "home." Sweet and elflike, Grandma Mary toddled along obediently, gazing at the new surroundings with the confused expression of a child who's suddenly awakened in an unfamiliar place. She clutched at her time-honored white sweater draped around her shoulders, held together by her favorite sweater clasp—a gold butterfly studded with red and blue rhinestones.

"Hmm," Grandma Mary muttered when she noticed an elderly man walking down the hall, talking to a parakeet perched on his finger. But when she saw a hamster encased in a plastic ball, rolling down the hall, she was moved to wide-eyed silence. When she spotted a woman sitting in a court-yard off a day room stroking and talking to the big, orange cat in her lap, Mary stopped to take a longer look. Her eyes gleaming, she remarked, "Hmmmh! Well, I'll be!" Delighted, her smile widened, revealing the dentures she had "polished just for this outing," as she had told us on the drive here. Suddenly, wanting to pet the cat, Mary tugged away from our bolstering hold on her arms. Dianne let her lead the way to the cat, and we waited as Grandma Mary approached the woman, who was already offering up the cuddly creature—a tawny orange animal, whose plump, soft body was greatly enhanced by his thick, long-haired, shiny coat. The drowsy cat looked perfectly content to be passed on from one adoring set of arms to the next. In fact, the regal feline looked as if such attention was his royal birthright. "What a gorgeous kitty you are," Mary crooned in a grandmotherly style as she gently but energetically petted the fat, fluffy feline.

After giving her a few minutes to fuss over the cat, Dianne patiently redirected her grandmother. "Okay, now we're going this way again, Grandma," she told Mary, who turned her head of tightly permed gray curls in our direction. It was clear that while Mary's pensive hazel eyes vaguely recognized Dianne as one of her grandchildren—just which grandchild this was she couldn't be sure. But when Mary glanced up at me, it was obvious she had no inkling at all of who I was, in spite of our earlier introductions. Her small frown and confused muttering told us she clearly wondered where we were taking her—and why. Grandma Mary has Alzheimer's.

We weren't all that Mary questioned. She was obviously puzzled over the sight of a shaggy little dog sprawled on the lobby floor. "Josie?" she asked, as though the pet could be a familiar one. When Mary was placed in Hillcrest, the nursing facility where she had lived for a year prior to this move, her precious little Pekinese, "Josie," had to go live with Dianne. Grandma Mary now looked hopeful as she took in the sight of the dog on the floor. Barely visible under all his black fur, his dark eyes peeked out at her. The little dog lifted his head to her, his tail waving an excited hello. "Nope," she concluded. "But you look just like her!"

A lot in life seemed, if not peculiar, then "almost" or "similar" or "sort of familiar" to Grandma Mary these days—as it had for the past several years. "Somebody tell Sam to come and get me," she ordered to no one in particular. Sam, her husband of more than fifty years, had passed away more than a decade ago. As happens with Alzheimer's patients, Mary sometimes forgets significant information such as this.

"Look, Grandma," Dianne enthused, pointing to the large garden area where several seniors were tending to the plants. "Just like the flower beds you used to have! And you can plant your favorite bulbs!" Mary dully made eye contact with Dianne—and again tried to determine which of her grandchildren this was guiding her through this curious place. She had such trouble remembering things. All the medications she was taking made things even foggier—but this didn't stop her from recognizing the large deep crimson rose. "Oh, look!" Mary exclaimed, her face lighting up as she headed towards the giant flower to get a closer look. "It's an Ingrid Bergman rose, all right." She examined the exquisite flower and then explained, "Of *all* the roses, they have the most beautiful fragrance! And they're among the largest, too."

The sight of her grandmother gently fondling the rose and then breathing in its ample sweet fragrance brought tears to Dianne's eyes. When her mother passed away, her grandmother's care had become Dianne's responsibility. Since Grandma Mary requires around-the-clock attention and since Dianne works full time, a nursing facility seemed to be the only solution. But the first nursing home Dianne had selected proved to be a poor one for Grandma Mary. Seeing how drastically her grandmother's physical and mental health declined after spending just a year there, Dianne began an intense search for an alternative.

Finding a place for her grandmother took on supreme importance—and wasn't as easy as Dianne thought it would be. As she investigated and researched care for the elderly, Dianne was surprised to learn there are "three plagues" of geriatric institutional life: loneliness, helplessness, and boredom—none of which are cured by pills, sterile halls, or solitary living. Unfortunately, these "plagues" accurately described the last nursing home Grandma Mary had been in, and as a result, her beloved grandmother was so unhappy that she had actually remarked that her life was "not worth living." Her granddaughter was determined to make certain Grandma Mary didn't fall victim to any of these afflictions again.

"It was all too impersonal," Dianne said, referring to the Hillcrest Seniors Home. "Grandma needs around-the-clock nursing care, but that doesn't mean she should be deprived of a real life. I think we forget that when seniors enter a nursing home, they leave a big world behind, and they pay a big price for that. The longer Grandma was at Hillcrest," Dianne confided, "the more distant she became. Her health grew worse.

I knew it wasn't just that she was getting older. I could really understand how unhappy she was in that place. I didn't even like to have to go there to visit. It was sterile, empty, lifeless."

I could relate. When I was a young girl, my grandparents often asked me to go with them to visit a couple of their friends who resided in a nursing home. Perhaps they thought it would be nice for the seniors in the home to have a young person around and that it would be good for a young girl to be around seniors. I found it frightening and absolutely detested going there, even if it was with grandparents whom I adored.

The nursing home was a sterile place where everyone looked so pale, so frail, so ill, so unhappy. And it seemed to me that everyone was asleep much of the time. That didn't seem normal to me, a young girl of nine. Why would they want to sleep when they could escape this place and go for walks with family and friends? And why shouldn't their pets be allowed to visit? I couldn't imagine being separated from my dog. Many of the rules seemed odd. Visitors were asked to be "quiet," as though the sounds of people talking and laughing were intrusive and disturbing. And though it was acceptable to bring cut flowers to residents, no plants were allowed. A live tree sat in the corner of my room at home and had been there from the time I could remember. Plants and trees were supposed to be *everywhere*.

I just knew the seniors home was a terribly stultifying place for those who lived there—even if the residents, like Mary, didn't always know just exactly where they were. And I could imagine how terrible it must be to leave your own home (I could never imagine giving up my room), leaving behind your pets, the people you loved, and all your familiar and precious belongings to come to a small place with none of your own things, or at least nothing more than a picture or two.

And so my interest had been piqued when Dianne told me she'd found an "alternative" for her grandmother. "Grandma went from the responsibilities of caring for her home to Hillcrest," Dianne explained. "Hers was a home that stored a lifetime of memories. It was a home with plants she loved to care for, an ample feather bed with a massive, intricately detailed cast iron frame — an old family heirloom — where her Pekinese slept at her feet for a decade. It was in a neighborhood she had lived in for years, a place where faces were familiar and time-honored — like the mailman who handed her the mail and neighbors checked up on her, and the neighborhood kids stopped by to sell cookies or to beg for some. It was a place where she reigned as Lord and Lady when family and friends came to visit. Suddenly, Grandma is without any of this, without any of the people or responsibilities that gave her purpose. But not anymore!"

If Grandma Mary often looked lost as we made our way through these halls, Dianne, alight with hope, looked like she believed her grandmother was finally found! The "alternative" is an Eden Alternative Care Facility, a senior's nursing facility designed to create an environment where seniors can have a "life," while still receiving full-time care. This home, like the other Eden Alternative Care Facilities, was started by Dr. William Thomas. A Harvard-educated family practitioner and geriatrician, Dr. Thomas says that Eden is about "care for the soul, care for the spirit, things that don't come on a medical cart or in a pill." Eden is a lot less like a hospital and a lot more like a home, complete with pets, a garden, and even kids — a place where the "three plagues" aren't likely to find a host. Loneliness is warded off through close and continuing hands-on contact and interaction with pets and people, offering companionship. Residents are allowed to care for the pets and plants, abating helplessness. Boredom is combated by allowing the spontaneity of children, small animals, and stimulating activities. Here residents experience a truer sense of "home," one filled with love and laughter, pets, plants, and people. It's a sharp contrast from the nursing home I had visited with my grandparents—and from the one where Grandma Mary had spent the past eleven months.

Mary Whitney has resided at Eden for a year now. Dianne and I often talk about how her grandmother is doing, and on occasion I go with Dianne to visit Mary. The changes in her are remarkable, as evidenced in Dianne's comment: "When I went to visit Grandmother at Hillcrest, I'd sit with her and politely ask simple questions, most of which had little meaning, like, 'What did you watch on TV last night?' Now, from the minute I see Grandma, she's nonstop chatter, she's so filled with life again. And the doctors have cut down the dosage of her antidepressant medications. What a change!"

Many things have changed in Mary's life. For one, she's in love with "Auggie" as he is affectionately known—one of the several cats-in-residence. The portly yellow tabby stays close to Mary, sleeping on her bed near her feet. He can also be found rubbing against her as she tends to her roses. And, Mary has drawers filled with the things visiting children bring her—each of them includes a story she loves to tell and has no difficulty remembering. The children who go to the adjoining kindergarten trail through the halls heading for the playground on their way to recess every day. Like Auggie, one of them has singled Mary out. A lively, rambunctious little boy approached her one day and declared, "You must be *really* old!" Much more alert than she'd been months before when she'd first arrived at Eden, Mary scowled down at him, then couldn't help but smile. "Yes, I am really old, all right," she agreed, and then said good-naturedly, "and you're really rude to mention it." Knowing children are innocent of their remarks, she was smiling as she said it. The little boy, Toby, who had a permanently mischievous little gleam in his eyes, smiled and shrugged, "Sorry." From that day on, he showed Mary all sorts of treasures: a marble, an action figure, a rock from his pocket. Occasionally, he'll permanently donate one of the treasures to her—or gift her with a picture he'd drawn just for her. And so Mary found herself with a drawer that was a treasure chest of Toby's offerings—a drawer made necessary by their need of each other.

Mary also makes certain she makes it to the bay-view window come recess time to "keep an eye on that little boy, Toby." Today, as Mary remembers her latest gift from her little admirer, she points out the new picture on her wall. "Toby—you know, the little scamp who comes to play in the yard outside, gave it to me," she says, shaking her head in mock exasperation. "He's full of mischief, that one, always pulling a little girl's ponytail or playing pranks on a playmate. He's all boy, that one!" Mary chuckles as she stares at Toby's latest masterpiece, some sort of vehicle and space creatures. "It's really good for such a little boy, don't you think?" she declares. He wanted to win her heart. He did: She is his biggest fan.

Looking at Mary Whitney today, with a cat to feed, the season's roses to prune, and a child who "needs overseeing," it's easy to see that Mary not only has a new home, but a new life—one worth living. And though she often misses her late husband Sam, she no longer asks where he is. Now more alert and mentally clear, she mentions him with love but is no longer "searching" for him.

Grandma Mary is well-suited for Eden. And Eden for her. Her vibrancy, her shining eyes, and her attention to her appearance show what "care of the soul" does for a person. It's what Eden has done for Mary Whitney—given her a place and space where she is encouraged to live a meaningful existence and not just wait out her life. Whether we are eight or eighty, *being* loved and cared for is vital to our health and happiness. *Giving* love and caring for others is just as essential.

Dianne's recognition of her beloved grandmother's unhappiness and pain created suffering for her, too, spurring her to seek the best possible solution. Her exhaustive search demanded nothing less than finding a setting that would offer care of the body as well as care of the soul. The setting at Eden produced a pearl Dianne regards as priceless—a restored sense of vibrancy and purpose for Grandma Mary.

Certainly, the desire to uplift the spirit of others is an indication of one's own happy spirit—a spirit that knows joy, health, and kindness. May we always seek to extend this charity of spirit to everyone—regardless of age.

The Lovers' Fight

"Life isn't a matter of milestones, but moments."
— ROSE KENNEDY

On our way to the airport, my daughter and I found ourselves traveling behind a car with two very animated passengers inside of it.

On the passenger side, a woman pressed herself against the door on her side of the car, practically leaning out the window. It appeared to me that she was rejecting whatever the driver—who was visibly upset—was saying. Her husband shook his head from side to side, shaking his fist in the air, and from time to time bobbing his head in the direction of his wife, as if to punctuate his tirade. Observing them made me uneasy. I took note of the fact that my daughter was gazing intently in their direction. She'd just recently gone through a breakup with her boyfriend and was in the midst of the initial heartbreak of it all. I was feeling particularly protective of her bruised feeling, and certainly didn't want anything to stir up any painful memories. Trying to lighten the impact of witnessing such conflict, I teased, "Think they're just arguing over whose turn it is to cook dinner?"

My daughter, nineteen at the time, looked at me in total amazement. "Why would you assume they're arguing, Mother?" she chided. "They are totally lovers! These two aren't wasting time arguing over whose turn it is to cook dinner!"

Surprised and interested in this completely different viewpoint, I asked, "Lovers? How do you figure that?"

"Well, just look at them, Mom," she directed. "The guy's girlfriend is resting against the door on her side of the car because she's got her legs stretched out on the seat. When he's not making a point, he's probably rubbing her feet. And look how happy they are. The boyfriend is using his hands to express himself passionately, and he keeps moving his head from side to side, all in her direction, as if he's just drawn towards her. They're probably planning something wonderful or discussing the fun of some trip they just got back from—or maybe even sharing something funny about their friends."

"Sorry, Jennifer, I just don't see it that way," I said.

Jennifer advised, "Keep an open mind, Mom."

"Let's check it out," I suggested.

"Okay," she said. Jennifer was so sure that she was right about the two people in the car in front of us, she wagered, "Whoever is wrong has to cook dinner."

I was so sure that I was right, I willingly conceded, "Deal!"

Curious to solve the mystery of whose perception was accurate, as we stopped at the stop sign where they were turning right and we were turning left, Jennifer and I made certain to get a better look. My husband and wife and Jen's boyfriend and girlfriend were, in fact, two men! The driver wore his hair short, the passenger wore his shoulder length. They were eating and laughing. Just two regular guys, together at lunch hour, coming or going somewhere, enjoying each other's company, maybe telling jokes or discussing a movie they had seen! We had both been wrong about their relationship, though Jen had no doubt been right about one thing: These two probably weren't wasting time arguing over whose turn it was to cook dinner!

As we both joined in laughter at our discovery, my dear daughter informed me, "Mom, I'm more right than you are, which means we're eating out!"

An old time adage, "1 + 1 = 3," implies that the synergy of two can alter one's perspective and that it's an added benefit. It's an even bigger premise than "two heads are better than one," although even that can be helpful in seeing detail and nuance necessary to constructing a more precise picture of life. Certainly "two heads are better than one" was helpful to the two of us that day: If I had been traveling alone, I would have stayed behind the two travelers, convinced they were having an argument. If my daughter had been traveling alone, chances are she too would not have been motivated to see the other motorist any differently than her initial notion of the rapture of two lovers. We both would have been wrong.

But perhaps even more important, though she and I were traveling together, if I had not been sensitive to her anguish and concerned how this encounter of a "couple arguing" would feel to her heart, neither of us would have been opened to our discovery. We each would have remained locked in our separate worlds, each clinging to our separate paradigms—both inaccurate: 1 + 1 = 2 is also possible.

Synergy implies a heartfelt willingness to consider the feelings of others, and to care about others, a compassion for how they are doing and faring. It is this sensitivity to the well-being of others that we open to life's bigger truths. It is then that we are able to more clearly see things as they really are, giving each of us the pearl of an entirely new and much more accurate perspective.

Consider the implications of 1 + 1 = 3 on a universal level!

Snowy Bird

"There is one happiness in life, to love and be loved."
—GEORGE SAND

Visiting a bird sanctuary one sunny Sunday afternoon, my husband, David, and I strolled through the aviary at a leisurely pace, stopping to feed the various birds and to pet those who were comfortable with the attention. I was coaxing one to warm up to the idea of sitting on my wrist, when my attention was drawn to a young man in the distance with a white bird perched on his fingers. As he moved the bird up and down, the bird got into the spirit of things, lifting his little wings up and down in perfect rhythm with the man's movements. The man gave a little signal, and the bird began to swing around the man's fingers, as if a circus acrobat. Enchanted, I went over to see the beautiful white bird perched on the finger of the attendant.

Reading the attendant's name on his badge, I said, "Hi, Marty. Great bird. What kind is it?"

"This is Snowy Bird," Marty replied. "He's an umbrella cockatoo." The cockatoo was snow white in color, a regal-looking bird with a high plume of feathers fanning from the crown of his head. But there was one exception to his majestic appearance. Snowy Bird had no feathers on his chest. Jarred by seeing this beautiful and obviously talented bird with such a raw and featherless chest, I asked Marty, "What happened? Did he have mites?"

Marty shook his head and explained, "No, Snowy Bird plucks out all the feathers on his chest himself. Two years ago his owners had to move out of the state and felt they could no longer care for him, so they brought him here. Quite simply, Snowy Bird is heartbroken. He still hasn't stopped pining for them. One of the ways he mourns his lost owners is to pluck the feathers from his chest."

I hadn't considered that a bird could "pine"—nor that it would miss a particular owner to the point of never forgetting her. "And Snowy Bird *still* hasn't gotten over it?" I asked, feeling for this beautiful little bird with an aching, empty heart. "Well," Marty explained, "whatever it is that goes on in Snowy Bird's head or heart, he is still missing them."

By now David had joined us, and we were observing the bird. David held out his finger for Snowy Bird to step onto, but Snowy Bird wanted no part of it and backed cautiously away. "C'mon over, little guy," David coaxed. "You sure are a pretty bird." The bird deliberately turned his head away from David. Then, looking at me, Snowy Bird began clawing the air, a motion I interpreted as his wanting to perch on my hand. Once again David put his finger up to the bird, hoping the bird might now be ready to perch on his hand. Once again Snowy Bird turned away from David and once again gestured for me to take him. So I put my finger up next to the attendant's hand. Instantly, Snowy Bird leaped from Marty's fingers and up onto my wrist.

Snowy Bird wasted no time making his way up my arm. Scuttling up the length of it, he perched on my shoulder, then nestled there, rubbing his head back and forth against my neck. I reached up and gently stroked Snowy Bird's soft silky feathers, comforting him with baby talk. Snowy Bird loved this and continued to rub his head against my neck, back and forth, back and forth. Leaning his little body taut against my neck, Snowy Bird then buried his head inside the collar of my shirt and cooed sweetly, "I'm Snowy Bird . . . I'm Snowy Bird."

My heart went out to him.

My face must have registered surprise at hearing the bird speak these words, and most especially in the sweet yet forlorn way the little bird cooed them. Reading my look of surprise, the attendant informed me, "We hear Snowy Bird say his name every couple of weeks, especially when he's stroked in that manner by someone who looks and sounds like you. It must be a similar look and sound to his previous owner—or at least Snowy Bird thinks so." Turning to look at the bird, whose head was still inside my collar, Marty added, "Here at the aviary we all give Snowy Bird all the love we can, but even so, just any love won't do. It's that special someone Snowy Bird misses—someone who looks and sounds like you."

Love, deepened by cherished experiences, *remembers*. As Snowy Bird pines with continual devotion to bring back a love and closeness he once knew, he reminds us that love is vital to all of us, even to umbrella cockatoos. Even in spite of its loss, it continues to seek itself.

What if everyone—including our little creature friends— didn't need to be loved as much as we do, in the way we each do? Luckily, we live in a world that needs love. In fulfilling our own need to love, we fulfill the need of others to be loved.

Snowy Bird's suffering was not for naught: His willingness to nuzzle into the neck of a perfect stranger and sing his name in his melancholy way garnered him a pearl. Today, Snowy Bird has a new owner to love—someone who looks and sounds just like me.

The Ambassador

*"Every forest branch moves differently in the breeze,
but as they sway, they connect at the roots."*

—RUMI

Sitting in his hospital bed on Christmas Eve, surrounded by "his three girls"—his wife, Carolyn, and daughters, Nancy and Cheryl—Ted Larsen reached out to receive their gift, a beautifully hand-wrapped package addressed simply, "Dad." His eyes filled with humility and gratitude, he thanked "his girls" even before unwrapping their offering.

Carefully and ever so slowly he removed the exquisite silver and gold paper—a gift-wrap chosen with the utmost deliberation. At the sight of the delicate, white photo album, his smile widened and his expressive blue eyes grew moist. Once again he thanked them for their generosity.

Savoring his every move, Nancy watched as her father reverently opened the album to the first page, filled with anticipation of what he would find there. Upon seeing that it was a picture of him as a small boy, Ted lowered his head to get a closer look at the lad in the photo and the caption: "There once was a boy." He chuckled and then read the words out loud, "There once was a boy."

Looking up at his girls, he shook his head playfully and cajoled, "You girls!" but quickly turned his attention to the album, eager to see what image await him on the next page. It was a picture of his wife as a little girl with the caption: "And a girl. . . ." This made him look to his wife, smile provocatively, and tease, "And what a girl!"

The next page showed "the boy" and "the girl" as a young couple in love, and on the following page, they were posed at the altar on their wedding day. Each page, each picture, brought a new smile. This gift brought Ted Larsen much delight. Then, the caption: "It's a girl!" Now Ted's merriment turned wistful and the eyes that had shown him fifty-four years' worth of life, misted over. Not at all self-conscious about these tears, he allowed them to slowly make their way down his face and drop onto the shoulders he raised to absorb them so as not to dampen the precious document he held in his hands. Clouding his eyes, the tears made the pictures seem fuzzy, so Ted lowered his head a bit more to get a better look at the young and oh so radiant first-time father proudly cradling a newborn Nancy in his arms. The next photo was much the same, except in this one the proud young father was holding baby number two, the third member on the dream team, "his girls."

Ted eagerly turned the pages of his new keepsake and with each one relived the memory anew. The three women quietly stole glances at one another—but tried not to, for fear the compassion of their shared pain would trigger their own tears—which would distract from the power of the happy memories bouncing around in these moments. Moments that right now belonged to the husband. And to the father. And to the ill man's chance to absorb this happiness and draw strength from it. "My girls," he repeated, smiling, nodding his head as if to confirm it.

Clearly "his girls" had brought this man much joy. Much contentment.

The album's heartfelt review of their life as a family also included pictures of all the big occasions, family vacations and holidays through the years, and even the family pets—Snowflake, the cat, and Prissy, their cocker spaniel. As Ted continued turning pages, engrossed in each snapshot, Nancy studied both her father's face and the photos he examined so carefully, so slowly, drinking in the sight of a dad who had given her good reason to love him so much—a dad who was her staunch supporter and friend for all these years. Glancing down at the photo he now studied, Nancy saw the image of a robust Ted aglow with pride as she stood beside him, grinning from ear-to-ear, draped in cap and gown with her high school diploma in her hand. The picture reflected just what she'd always known to be true: Her father was a good-natured, hearty, and self-confident man, a man who loved his family and knew how to express it.

She never doubted that he loved her, and always she knew he was happy with her and proud of her. As she was of him. An ever-present daddy, he was in fact, her hero. She need but look at the photos of the two of them together wherein she always leaned into him—his total acceptance was a given. She saw this not only in the picture of her high school graduation, the same was true when she was a gap-toothed seven-year-old the night of a school play, a beaming college graduate, and the independent, sophisticated, and worldly working girl being honored at a company awards banquet. Always there, he was always her devoted fan and benevolent protector.

Nancy watched as her father came to the last page of the album. It was a photo of that same stalwart man with "his girls" just a year before. The man she viewed studying that picture was now a pale shadow of his former self.

Six months earlier, Nancy's father had been diagnosed with cancer. He had hardly been sick a day in his life. The doctors said they could do nothing. The news shocked the whole family.

Now thin and weak, staring at the final photo with a peculiar blend of contentment and longing in his eyes, he appeared disappointed that the photos had ended.

Ted closed the album, his hands still clutching it tightly, as he looked up at "his girls." He closed his eyes and simply smiled. This the gracious man knew was more powerful than anything he could ever say. It was a moment of perfect love.

It was Ted Larsen's first day in the hospital. And his last. He died a few minutes later.

Now suddenly her world was upside down, turned inside out. For weeks afterward, even months, Nancy pondered the questions, "How could Daddy die—and so suddenly—he was only fifty-four? Could life be so fragile, so unpredictable, so uncertain?" And if it could be so, what was she to make of this—what lesson, what message, must she take from the experience of her father's sudden and untimely death? It was a time of great confusion for Nancy, a time when the ache in her head and heart was a physical pain—and so intense. She knew not if the clamoring going on inside her skull and chest was because she felt loss or because she was lost, and the noise was a calling—a certain something beckoning, begging for her attention, tugging at her in an effort to guide her, direct her. Though she never settled on a term for what seemed to fluctuate between a spiritual longing and simply a sadness deeper than she had ever known, it was a bewilderment that would cause her to assess her life. And though she didn't know it at the time, it would send her on a journey that would last seven years.

At twenty-nine, Nancy Larsen, a five-foot-ten inch dark-haired beauty, had close family ties, was in love, lived in a luxurious home, and had friends in every major city throughout the United States—and several countries to boot. Armed with a master's degree and an excellent job with American Airlines, she had planned to move up within her company; everyone knew it was but a matter of time. Her future looked bright. Until this moment.

Now Nancy Larsen no longer felt sure about anything except of her own mortality. She could not escape the question, *If I were to die tomorrow, how should I live today?* She found the question invasive, but because it pervaded seemingly her entire life, she tried to understand what it meant. "What am I supposed to be getting?" she asked. "Is there something wrong with my life in the way I'm living it now? How can I feel so complete one day and so empty the next? Are my feelings rational? Typical? Why do I suddenly feel 'misplaced'?"

She looked around at others, thoughtfully scrutinizing her friends, coworkers, and associates. She found them all to be good, hardworking people, but missing "a certain spark in their eyes, a certain happiness in their hearts." She hadn't noticed this before. Why now? She examined her social circle and concluded that it was "interesting, fast-moving, exciting, and never at a loss for fun"—and yet, the appeal for her was gone, replaced by an emptiness—one that gnawed at the corners of her consciousness and all but devoured her every waking moment. Worse, it demanded her hungry heart search for those answers, no matter how elusive they might be.

At first she thought her agony was over the loss of her beloved father, but she slowly began to understand that a bigger longing was brewing and that the question wouldn't be going away anytime soon. Even on those days when she felt at peace with the absence of her father and his friendship in her daily life, still the haunting whisper demanded: "So if I were to die tomorrow, how should I live today?" Facing down the question scared her, but running from it scared her even more.

Squaring off, Nancy made a very important decision: She would take a backward step in her career in order to take a forward step towards her soul.

Resigning from the more time-consuming duties of her administrative and supervisory job, Nancy took a position as a flight attendant so she would have more time and freedom to appease the demand to answer the question of how exactly should she be living her life today—so that it might feel purposeful, fulfilling, truly lived. She used the time to go back to school to pursue doctoral studies, spent time with family and close friends, attended workshops and conferences, and traveled to places she felt compelled to visit. Spurred on by a yearning not yet named—let alone understood—Nancy journeyed and journeyed.

And oh, what an extraordinary adventure it was. She lived with the Hopi Indians in New Mexico, as well as the Incas in the Andes of Peru. She trekked through humid jungles, sailed the oceans, trudged through deserts, and scaled glacier-topped mountains. In her quest for the answer to how to live life "for today," she looked for its presence in the bitter cold of the former Soviet Union and in the ache of compassion she felt for a little orphaned girl she adopted in Sri Lanka. She literally journeyed to the four corners of the earth—from the US to Tibet from the Philippines to El Salvador—to find an answer to quell her restless desire as to how she might live today as importantly and purposely as though it was to be her last. For seven years.

Her quest, while such an outward excursion, had also been a voyage to the depths of her soul. It left her heart forever changed and her values powerfully transformed.

Different people, different cultures, different walks of life, different ideas and beliefs. So different, yet the same. Unity. It was all about unity. Giving. Sharing. Helping one another.

It was from that vantage point of a newfound abiding respect and love for all humanity that magic happened: She was filled with an open innocence and childlike wonder. The ache in her head and heart subsided, replaced by an empathy for the well-being of peoples everywhere. It was from this place of purity and love that Nancy was open and receptive to the answer to the question that had besieged her since her father's death.

Her discovery was startling in its simplicity. The answer to the deep, yet basic, esoteric, yet very practical question of "how should I live my life today" could be found in this simple precept: Serve others; see a need and do what you can to help.

Service to others was central to how she should live her life.

Overjoyed and empowered by the simplicity and wonder of it all, Nancy knew she had to share this gift with others so that they too would experience the same meaning—and magic— she had. Filled with passion and purpose, she set out to let people know what awaited them. Starting in the arena she knew best, she decided that an in-flight video—one that would inspire travelers to "make a difference" was simple and easy. Emphatic, she pitched her idea at the corporate level.

No one was interested.

"How am I to reach others?" she asked herself, confused by the lack of enthusiasm she'd met. 'By example' an inner voice clearly responded. "Live YOUR life serving others."

And so she did. Resuming her full-time work with the airlines, she "lived today"—each day—with a focus on serving others. Through her connection with the airlines, she delivered humanitarian aid and goodwill everywhere her company's route took her. And more. She volunteered literally hundreds of hours escorting orphans from one end of the world to new homes in another. She solicited every tribe, troop, and organization, pleading for everything from medical supplies to food, clothes, and toys for orphaned children living in the most remote regions of the globe. She pleaded with doctors and other experts to share their expertise with those who needed medical attention and their services. Hours upon hours upon hours for the next fourteen years she served!

Example is a powerful teacher. And a most persuasive one. Her selfless acts, and her obvious joy and peace in giving them, have spoken more persuasively than any proposal could possibly hope to. Today, nearly two decades later, the outreach of Nancy Larsen Rivard has spawned Airline Ambassadors—a nonprofit organization that has a membership of more than two million and growing. What began as a one-woman show and then became a handful of volunteers—"ambassadors"—now reaches literally millions and millions the world over.

Airline Ambassadors, now with most major airlines fully entrenched in such missions, has hand delivered millions of dollars of humanitarian aid to children in twenty-one countries and escorted thousands of orphans to new homes, aided thousands more needing medical care, and involved nearly a million youths in cross-cultural friendships worldwide.

"There once was a boy" so capable of loving a family—most especially a little dark-haired girl—that his absence would send that girl in search of refilling the painful hole that his departure left within her heart.

Her seed of sorrow was cultivated into a pearl of coordinated action for humanitarian assistance. The result is Airline Ambassadors, an entity that creates miracles in the lives of others—while transforming the lives of those who give, as well. Like an entire string of pearls, the outreach of Airline Ambassadors forms a circle of service of humanitarian assistance and activism, linking person to person, country to country, continent to continent, around the globe. Conceived in pain and born of grief over losing a young father she adored, Nancy Rivard leaves the most priceless gift of all. In helping others, we live "today" with supreme purpose—an act that sets our compass in the direction of the most profound journey of all—the path to our inner self, to our own soul, the pearl within.

An Excellent Example

"In the middle of difficulty lies opportunity."
—ALBERT EINSTEIN

I looked at the artsy greeting card in my hand, remarkable for its vivid and vibrant color schemes and its surrealistic images. The exquisite card, one of a set of ten, had lain in my drawer for months, reserved for "special occasions." Today, as I searched the drawer for a card to send for just such an occasion, the card captured my attention. Thumbing through the other cards in the series, I admired each unique, original cover design, so elegantly simple and at the same time complex—as though the picture held a lovely secret, but one the artist refused to give up. The greeting cards had been given to me as a token of appreciation for speaking to a professional organization holding their monthly meeting at St. Madeline Sophie's Center—a center for developmentally disabled adults. When the director of the center presented the cards to me, she made it clear that I was receiving something special by saying, "This is an excellent example of the work of one our most gifted artists."

"Aren't these cards exquisite?" I said, holding one up for Tina, a member of my office staff, to see.

"They really are," she agreed, genuinely impressed. "Who's the artist?"

"I don't know," I remarked, and then flipping the card over and noting the artist's name, I said, "It's by Mark Rimland." I hadn't heard of Mark Rimland, but the name *Rimland* was familiar. "Rimland, Rimland," I pondered the name out loud. About ten years ago I had been involved in a video project with Dr. Bernard Rimland, a research psychologist for the navy. As I recalled, Dr. Rimland had an autistic son. Could there be a connection? I mentioned the possibility to Tina.

"Does it say anything else about the artist?" she asked.

I flipped the card over again and read out loud: "Original designs are created by the artists of St. Madeline Sophie's Center. . . . They have gifts to share and contributions to make to our society. This art is one excellent example of these gifts."

I decided to call Dr. Rimland to see if perhaps there was a connection. As it turned out, there definitely was.

"Healthy lungs," Bernard and Gloria Rimland both agreed proudly when their son, Mark, was born wailing. But when their baby boy hadn't stopped screaming long after he'd come home, months later to be exact, their parental pride turned to concern. Soothing their newborn seemed impossible. Little Mark resisted cuddling, in fact, he seemed to detest it. Exhausted most of the time, Bernard and Gloria were only able to get their son to sleep when they placed him in a carriage and pushed it back and forth, bouncing it over a yardstick they had taped to the floor. But it was his parents who were sleep deprived, not Mark. He seemed to need very little sleep.

Aside from being inconsolable, Mark appeared to be an exceptionally bright infant. He skipped crawling altogether and walked and talked when he was only eight months of age. Most especially startling was his ability to mimic what he heard on the TV or radio—verbatim. At only eight months old, he could remember and perfectly articulate complete phrases such as, "Come on, let's play ball." But what was most unusual, and disturbing, was that their son seemed oddly disconnected from his parents' touch, warmth, and caretaking. It was as though he were unable to grasp that he was dearly loved. He also seemed incapable of showing affection in return and acted as though affection was unimportant to him. They found this unsettling, as you can imagine. They were also puzzled and needed answers. And so the search began.

One day, as Mark's mother watched her son vacantly recite nursery rhymes, she remembered reading about similar behavior in a college textbook. She and Bernard searched the garage for the old textbook and, finding it, discovered it described their son point by point: Mark had "infantile autism." Though he held a Ph.D. in psychology, it was the first time Bernard had ever seen or heard the term. Yet, the behavioral characteristics described in the textbook—uncontrollable tantrums, staring into space for hours on end, showing no interest in people, even parents and siblings—fit their son to a T. Other than the fact that autism afflicts five out of ten thousand children and "imprisons its victims in a world all their own," little else was known about autism. But it was enough to make Dr. Rimland realize that autism was a powerful monster—one that had seized his son.

This was the late 1950s, when the suggested treatment was to put an autistic child in an institution because it was believed that the child was unable to be mainstreamed into society and that his presence in the home would prove to be an over-whelming burden to the family. The Rimlands couldn't imagine living apart from their son. Instead, they took a hands-on approach: If Mark didn't know how to come to them, they would reach into their son's world.

In school Bernard had specialized in the methodology of behavioral science—what people believe to be true and why. In his position with the navy, he designed tests to measure a recruit's aptitude for various jobs. Research, proof, answers, and solutions were his passion. Now, he had a new cause. And an even greater reason to turn theory into practice. Intent on helping his son break out of the darkness of autism, Dr. Rimland fervently applied his skills to researching autism. Driven by his desire to tap into his son's world—to *know* his son—Dr. Rimland set out on a crusade to find out how he could enable connection and communication with little Mark.

Dr. Rimland decided to read everything he could find about autism—which was very little. He then began seeking out and talking with other parents of autistic children to learn of their experiences. It was slow going. He discovered that for the most part, parents of autistic children pretty much kept to them-selves. Though they desperately wanted to know how they could help their children, and because the literature and pro-fessional community were so limited, parents assumed that other parents, too, were at a loss on how to reach their children.

Knowing that it was crucial that parents of autistic children talk with each other about their children—share their experi-ences as parents of autistic children—Dr. Rimland founded the National Society for Autistic Children (now the Autism Society of America). This parent-support network proved useful and important. Now parents of autistic children had a spokesman, someone who knew firsthand what they were going through—someone who, like them, had an autistic child and was looking for hope. And, they also now had a spokesman who relentlessly sought answers.

The "answers" would come from the parents themselves as they shared what they were doing that stimulated interaction and connection with their own autistic children. Their contact and the body of information it produced was insightful and once again proved useful: Some parents *had* found ways to get their children to bond with them. And, to Dr. Rimland's great amazement, autism wasn't as generic as once thought. There were different kinds and degrees of autism. As importantly, some autistic children were not only capable of leading normal lives, but were also gifted, had remarkable talents and enormous aptitudes for learning.

This novel and significant information shed new light on autism and led Dr. Rimland to championing the rights of autistic children to get a public education.

The floodgates had been opened. Now unshackled from their guilt, parents with autistic children the world over began talking about their children. This intensity led to even more dramatic findings about autism, ones which soon caused professionals to acknowledge that autism is, in fact, a biological brain disorder and not caused by a lack of a mother's love—a theory that had heretofore been unchallenged. More fervent than ever, Dr. Rimland founded The Institute for Child Behavior Research (now the Autism Research Institute), an international clearinghouse on autism.

Through his efforts, the body of knowledge on autism was growing and unfolding. Dr. Rimland chronicled this groundbreaking work in *Infantile Autism: The Syndrome and Its*

Implications for a Neural Theory of Behavior, a landmark book altering the thinking of psychologists, psychiatrists, and other professionals in the field. Information produced enlightenment and public interest. Dr. Rimland was at the heart of it. And so was his son. Not only was Dr. Rimland the technical consultant for the movie *Rain Man,* his son, Mark, was one of the savants with whom Dustin Hoffman worked in preparing for his Academy Award–winning role.

And in the end, Dr. Rimland not only had championed a stunning breakthrough for parents and professionals everywhere, but also accomplished exactly what he had set out to do: he found a way to connect with his son.

Today, because of his father, Mark is no longer locked in a world of his own. Mark is not just a person who is afflicted with autism:

He is a son.

He is a brother.

He is a cousin.

He is an uncle.

He is a friend.

And he is a contributing member of our society.

Mark's particular disorder classifies him as an autistic savant, meaning that aside from his disabilities in communicating, he has extraordinary talent—as the greeting cards I held in my office attest. He is a brilliant and gifted artist. St. Madeline Sophie's Center thinks so, too. And the world is beginning to get a glimpse of this as well. More and more, Mark's work is being recognized and winning acclaim. His paintings have been exhibited in art shows; his illustrations grace cards as well as the pages of books (most recently, a children's book, *The Secret Night World of Cats*); he's been featured on *CBS This Morning,* on PBS, and other TV shows. His paintings sell in the thousands of dollars.

It's not just his awesome talent that makes this artist special. Mark Rimland is a vibrant young man with a quick smile, an engaging sense of humor, and a sharp wit. Though he looks somewhat like a younger and trimmer version of his father, he is very much his own person. Sitting at lunch with them, Mark reads the menu, mulls it over, often critiquing certain dishes. He is an attentive and eager listener, patient, and should a lull in the conversation occur, he is always ready to turn the conversation to his passion — art!

Ask him when he first realized he was good at art, and there will be a pat answer: "September 15, 1977. It was a Thursday." At this response, his father smiles wryly — few people could better appreciate and understand this classic response, typical of Mark's personality. When I asked Mark what his favorite piece of art was, he pointed to the picture shown on the next page. "An excellent example," he says matter of factly.

After our lunch, I watched as father and son walked away, arm-in-arm. Talking intently, each was engrossed in what the other had to say. It was a memorable scene — and a very loving one. Father and son, talking, laughing, *sharing* — just as Dr. Rimland had hoped.

The Rimlands' overwhelming frustration at their son's inability to grasp that they dearly loved him, as well as the sense of lonely isolation they experienced at Mark's being incapable of receiving their affection, drove Dr. Rimland to search for a way to connect with their autistic child. Not only did this result in the pearl of precious connection with Mark, it extended to a strand of pearls as countless parents of autistic children throughout the world are now able to experience mutually loving relationships with their children.

Considering that his original intent was simply to help his family find a way into Mark's world, it's a sweet irony that through his work he connected a world of families to their children and, because of it, they in turn share with us their gifts, talents, and contributions—their "examples of excellence."

"Japanese Birds" by Mark Rimland

Of Tiaras, Titles, and Trials

"The sky will bow to your beauty if you do."

—RUMI

A vision of exquisite beauty, Jacquelyn Mayer all but floated down the red carpeted runway, waving to a packed auditorium and a nationally televised audience—all of whom she held breathlessly captive at this annually awaited moment. Serenaded by the distinctive words of the song, "Here She Is, Miss America," her radiant, picture-perfect smile sparkled as brightly as the dazzling tiara perched regally atop her upswept hair. Jacquelyn had worked towards this moment with a single-minded passion—and her greatest dream had come true. If the photographers with their flashing lights, the swarm of television cameras, the enormous crowd of roaring, whistling, and cheering well-wishers, the enthusiastic hugs of fellow contestants, and the crown weren't enough to convince her it was real, Jacquelyn need only glance down at her sash to read the words: "Miss America, 1963."

"What will you do now? What will you do now?" reporters asked the young woman who had captured a most-coveted crown—as well as everyone's attention. Hesitantly—because although her dream had always been to be seen and to be heard, for what, she wasn't quite sure—she answered, "Well, I am a representative of my country, so I will be a spokeswoman." At the time, it was that simple.

It wouldn't always be so.

Seven years after the spectacular pinnacle of being crowned Miss America, Jacquelyn Mayer suffered a stroke.

In the stroke's aftermath, the woman who had strolled down the runway with such poise could no longer walk at all. The young beauty who had so easily fielded questions posed by judges and responded to the media with articulate eloquence could no longer talk at all. Suddenly and unexpectedly, Jacquelyn was faced with having to restore skills and the basic knowledge she'd once taken for granted and considered natural abilities. She would have to learn to walk again. She would have to learn words—and how to form them—all over again.

But other obstacles abounded. Rehabilitation was grueling and painful. And, immediately following her reign, she had married and had two children. They were young, and caring for herself had become more than she could handle; caring for her young children on top of that took her to the brink of exhaustion. Life seemed impossibly difficult and, especially, most unfair.

Despair set in and then hopelessness. She plummeted into a world of frustration, doubt, and insecurity. Robbed of her confidence, the bitter seeds of self-pity took root, and she turned inward and away from the people and public she loved. Though support, concern, and advice poured in from friends, admirers, and professionals, nothing it seemed could help her regain a foothold on life. Even with the love and support of her husband, Jacquelyn doubted if she even wanted to.

A child can be a patient if persistent teacher, and Jacquelyn was about to get a dose of motivation. Her ten-year-old son, Bill, who upon seeing his mother's attitude of apathetic hopelessness, offered the best suggestion. "You have to *do something*, Mom," the little boy said. "But what?" she asked, not really expecting the profound answer that was to follow.

"I don't know," the little boy answered, "but first you have to get up off your butt."

Her son's innocent and well-meant words struck a resounding chord of truth, a reality that Jacquelyn gratefully embraced. Realizing that she had fallen into a black hole of personal ineptness and helplessness, one so deep that even a young child noticed, Jacquelyn decided it was time to begin to dig out of her abyss. If the accident had created lemons, her children would be the sugar.

She enlisted their support and with their help, began the slow and arduous process of rebuilding her life. While her nine-month-old daughter, Kelly, learned to walk for the first time, Jacquelyn learned to walk for the second. Bill taught her things that she'd once taught him, like the alphabet and how to tie her shoes.

Day by day, week by week, month by month, Jacquelyn accepted the challenge to "make lemonade" from the lemons that had been heaped upon her—to accept the work of rebuilding her life. This included a shift of paradigms. Jacquelyn Mayer once told herself that she need only dream big enough and she could *have* whatever she wanted *from* life. But in working to overcome the debilitating results of the stroke—and her initial despondent and ineffectual response to it—Jacquelyn realized something different: She need only dream big enough and she could *give* whatever she wanted *to* life.

In giving, she received.

Just as challenge can lead us to live more fully, it can also cause us to bring conviction to what we have learned in our struggles. In carrying the crosses we have to bear, in overcoming the obstacles that are ours to endure, we gain a certain mastery in that which we have toiled through and risen above. The result is often a clear vision—a conviction—and a desire to help others do or achieve what we have.

Today, Jacquelyn Mayer has a cause that fills her with direction, motivation, inspiration, and purpose. Hard-won experience would grace her crown with a new pearl: experience by not only tribute, but also by tribulation. The result is spectacular! Her tiara and title now include a triumph put to good use: Jacquelyn is a representative for her country and its citizens, an ardent spokeswoman for the National Stroke Association and American Heart Association. She speaks throughout the world, sharing what she has learned with others so that they, too, might have the courage to overcome their obstacles and find renewed vibrance after setbacks as life-changing as a stroke. It's a victory worth crowning!

Her message encourages and inspires. People are in awe. "How did you do it? How did you do it?" everyone asks the revitalized beauty. Without hesitation—because she is quite sure of herself these days—Jacquelyn smiles her dazzling smile and says, "It's important to *do* something with your life. You have to start somewhere. A very special and wise little boy once put it to me this way: 'The first thing you have to do is get up off your butt!' "

Swede Style

"I used to be shy. You made me sing."

—RUMI

Stepping into the classroom, sixteen-year-old Susan White glanced up to survey the room, parting the dark veil of long brown hair her downcast gray eyes often used to conceal themselves. A quiet and demure little girl, she looked more like a thirteen-year-old than someone at the halfway mark of adolescence. "Susan White!" she lamented to her best friend. "How ordinary. There are nineteen other Susans in my school and six Whites—none of us related. I don't even have a name of my own. It's the pits being just an average nobody."

The pensive eyes of the "average nobody" darted from one empty seat to the next, looking for a place to sit, then narrowed in on the back of the room. There, not in the very back row, but close, sat

Donnie Watkins, a very versized, insecure boy who was not the type to call attention to himself in class. If she sat behind Donnie Watkins, she'd have a good chance of remaining anonymous and unnoticed—as usual. Susan headed for the desk, plunked her backpack on top of it, and slouched into her chair.

American history! The thought hardly excited the indifferent student. School held little appeal—especially a subject as dry as American history. Fishing around in her backpack, the teenager who shared her first name with nineteen other students in the school took out her notebook and pencil and then hung her backpack on the back of her seat. Laying the notebook and pencil on the desk in front of her, she studied them blankly, fidgeting with them so she had something to do with her hands. Even if it was the first day of a new semester, even if it was the beginning of a new set of classes and different teachers, and even if there was a good probability she could meet a few new faces, to Susan it was just another boring day of school. Boooring!

At a brisk clip the thirtyish teacher, his head full of auburn curls, came marching into the classroom. All smiles, the attractive man with the neatly trimmed beard and mustache hitched up the belt on his smartly tailored black dress slacks. Adjusting the psychedelic necktie he was wearing, he rolled the sleeves of his white shirt up to his elbows, briefly glanced at his colorful Swatch watch, and then turned to write his name on the board: "Mr. Swede." While the teacher prepared to begin class, Susan watched with curiosity, but when the handsome man turned around to face the students, she resumed her slouch, sinking down even farther in her chair.

As Mr. Swede handed out the class syllabus, she kept her eyes trained on her desk until her copy was handed to her. Then she feigned intent concentration on the curriculum it outlined so she would look interested. And busy. Too busy to be pulled into being asked a question. Way too busy for eye contact. School . . . so stressful. So boring. She wanted to be *anywhere* but in school. Anywhere. . . .

"Okay, class," Mr. Swede began with a confident smile and all the excitement of a teenager about to put the keys into the ignition of the first set of wheels for which he had the pink slip! Then, pedal to the metal, the lively teacher roared to life! His face animated, his eyes widened, his hands waving in the air, he launched into a series of lively anecdotes and accounts, all related to American history.

Susan peered around Donny, not enough so that the teacher could see her, but enough so that she could see him. On and on, Mr. Swede lectured, fielding questions with the same fervor he displayed as he called upon students. Susan sat in quiet awe of him, her own elusive and apathetic gaze sparked with unexpected interest. Trying to thwart any future disappointment, she assured herself it was just a matter of time and Mr. Swede would be like the rest of the teachers—dull, boring, predictable—and his class would be like the others—big words, dumb facts, information that was irrelevant to life, especially hers.

Three months passed, and still Mr. Swede maintained his enthusiasm, vigor, and *even* his academic appeal. Still, he loved teaching. Still, he genuinely liked his students. Still, he was excited about his subject matter. Still, he knew his subject so well that interesting facts just poured from him! There was no way the ordinary girl could deny she was nothing short of mesmerized by the extraordinary man. Susan White decided the teacher must be brilliant. Obviously he had chosen the right profession. The guy genuinely liked his job and was so obviously a happy person. Soon, the timid student began to look forward to each day; before taking his class, Susan would never have thought such a thing was possible. But something about Mr. Swede's passion and great gift for story-telling made history come alive for her. It wasn't long before she began raising her hand with questions or comments, forgetting to worry that people would notice her. Mr. Swede called on her, and when he did, he made Susan feel as if every comment was of great value and every question was an excellent one—and *all* were signs of her high intelligence. She was worthy. Capable. Likable. "Ms. Smith."

"Your midterm essay will be timed," Mr. Swede told the class when it came time for their exam. Pacing with his easy, confident manner before the chalkboard at the front of the room, he instructed, "You are to write all the facts you can remember about the Civil Rights Movement." Susan's eyes widened in delight as she sighed in nervous satisfaction. Putting her pencil to her paper, Susan began to write. She wrote, and wrote, and wrote—eighteen pages worth of writing, covering 256 facts.

As it turned out, Susan listed more facts than anyone else in the class was able to record.

For the remaining weeks in the semester, as Mr. Swede walked around the room while the class was doing their written assignments, the excellent teacher would pass her desk and pause to lean over and whisper, "Two hundred and fifty-six, just imagine!" Susan basked in the praise. She wasn't "just an average nobody" after all—or at least she wasn't in Mr. Swede's class! "Be sure to talk with the counselors about universities!" he encouraged. One time the history buff who had condensed centuries upon centuries of civilizations into the width of the blackboard, suggested, "You know, you could *teach* history. *You* could *be* a teacher. . . ."

A history teacher? Susan wondered about this prospect. There was a time when she would have never considered it: standing in front of class, teaching *history* of all things. Now she thought about what it might be like to know so much that she could be the class leader. What *would* it be like to have others admire her—like she looked up to Mr. Swede?

A teacher . . . The thought intrigued her. It would mean a big change of plans. Just this past summer she had concluded when she graduated from high school—if she graduated—she would get a job, even though she had no idea what kind of work she would do. But Mr. Swede believed in her and even thought she had the potential to be a history teacher!

A teacher . . .

If her admiration of Mr. Swede wasn't already recorded in the annals of time, it was sealed on the last day of the school year when the yearbooks came out. In hers, he wrote: "You have great promise. I hope you'll work hard, go to a fine university, and help change the world. If ever you doubt yourself, just remember, 'Two hundred and fifty-six!' "

Today Susan stands in front of a classroom of high school students—a history class—teaching. It is work for which she is obviously well suited. Two years ago she was named her state's Teacher of the Year and finished among the nation's top ten finalists—the best of the best of the best exemplary educators through the nation!

How did such an average nobody become such a somebody? "It's absolutely because of Mr. Swede," Susan admits, explaining, "I know how important it is that I project a dynamic energy, a zestful vitality, and an absolute brilliance, qualities my students will pay attention to and admire. Kids are more in need of models than critics. They need to feel liked. And special. I know how key these qualities are in reaching teens—especially the ordinary nobodies who sit in the back of the room and hope not to be noticed.

"I once heard the job of teaching described as, 'education is not the filling of a pail but the lighting of a fire,' and I know now how true that is. Having had Mr. Swede for a teacher, I understand the importance of knowing what it takes to turn youth on and desire to set goals for themselves.

"It's not as easy as it looks! Many times I get discouraged, worrying whether or not I'm making a difference in the lives of my students. I wonder if they know I care about them and how much I want them to find the class interesting, meaningful, and useful to their lives right now.

"Now I can look back and understand exactly what Mr. Swede was going through. When he encountered students like me—and I encounter them all the time—I know that while you smile and cajole on the outside, it's a torch of anguish within that fuels your desire to reach them." Susan smiles, her engaging gray eyes satisfied, and adds, "But whenever the job overwhelms me, whenever I doubt my ability to reach my students, and most especially when I encounter 'an average nobody' who gazes at me with apathetic eyes," she laughs at the memory of the girl she once was and continues, "I get out my high school yearbook. Recalling the affirming tone of someone who made a bigger difference in my life than anyone else, who encouraged me even more so than my parents—I read the words Mr. Swede wrote one day when I was just a little lost and bored student: 'You have great promise . . . work hard . . . change the world. If ever you doubt yourself, just remember, 'Two hundred and fifty-six!' Those words have been worth more miles than he will ever know!"

"Just an average nobody" has come a long way. Delivered from the apathy of low self-esteem, Susan began her journey to achievement fueled by the inspiration of Mr. Swede's belief in her. To inspire someone, to show them even a glimpse of their potential is a noble task. And a laborious one. But what beauty the world would have lost if no one were to dive to the ocean floor to reach the pearls that lay there in their tightly protected shells.

Sometimes, we, too, must dive in with a robust splash of inspiration and draw out the pearls of potential from their tightly protected shells—shells sometimes sealed by the view of themselves as "just an average nobody."

Mr. Swede was not only able to see the talent in an ordinary student—but he was able to help a shy, timid "average nobody" with a "very used" name discover the purpose within herself. May we all aspire to such leadership.

Carry Me

"All that we behold is full of blessings."
—WILLIAM WORDSWORTH

The nurse on the late night shift walked into her patient's room in the intensive care unit and checked on his IVs and heart monitors. The day before he'd suffered cardiac arrest. The seasoned caregiver sat down in the chair beside his bed to observe him for a moment, compassionately laying her hands upon his arm. She knew well the importance of caring and encouragement to patients in these critical first few days of a life-threatening crisis. Seeing him stir, she asked softly, "Are you awake?"

"Yes," he nodded. When he opened his eyes and looked over at her, his need for comforting so spoke to her heart that she asked him if he wanted her to pray with him. "Oh, yes," he murmured. And so she did.

Then, certain her patient would find added solace and strength from her favorite prose—one she *always* carried with her—the nurse withdrew a piece of paper from her pocket and read:

"One night a man had a dream. He dreamed he was walking along the beach with the Lord. Across the sky flashed scenes from his life. For each scene, he noticed two sets of footprints in the sand; one belonging to him, and the other to the Lord.

"When the last scene of his life flashed before him, he looked back at the footprints in the sand. He noticed that many times along the path of his life there was only one set of footprints. He also noticed that it happened at the very lowest and saddest times in his life.

"This really bothered him and he questioned the Lord about it. 'Lord, you said that once I decided to follow you, you'd walk with me all the way. But I have noticed that during the most trouble-some times in my life, there is only one set of footprints. I don't understand why when I needed you most, you would leave me.'

"The Lord replied, 'My precious, precious child, I love you and I would never leave you. During your times of trial and suf-fering, when you see only one set of footprints, it was then that I carried you.' "

Pausing to let her patient savor the heartfelt prose—and to dab at the tears it always brought to her eyes—the nurse then smiled and patted his hand. Carefully she refolded the well-worn paper and gently slid the essential and invaluable balm back into her pocket. Over the years she had witnessed its healing power and knew it proved to be as calming as any sedative she administered. "No matter how many times I read it, I still find it beautiful," she said, "such profound food for the heart and soul. It's called 'Footprints.' I wish I could tell you who wrote it, but I don't know who did."

"I do," the man replied, love-filled memories once again transporting him back in time. Thinking he wasn't fully conscious because of the medications he was being given, the nurse didn't give much thought to his comment. But Paul Powers, the patient, *did* know the author. She was his wife—as well as his professional partner, the mother of his children, and the love of his life.

The prose the nurse had read began as a love story—his own.

When Paul proposed to Margaret, some thirty years before, she was happy, yet hesitant. She and Paul had such different backgrounds. Margaret knew the choice of a husband was one of the most important decisions she would ever make. She asked herself the questions most brides-to-be pose to themselves. Could a marriage between them work? Doubts assailed her. Margaret felt that despite their shared values and faith, there remained obstacles to their happiness.

The day of the proposal they'd traveled to a conference as part of Paul's work with a youth ministry. Stopping at a nearby beach, they decided to take a walk along the shore to discuss marriage and its importance.

Walking along, one moment speaking seriously and the next laughing as they dashed in and out of the waves rolling onto the shore, they realized they were young and in love, filled with hopes and dreams. Still, Margaret had her doubts. What would her parents say? Was *she* ready to marry? Did she and Paul fully understand the responsibilities of marriage? Were they ready to commit their lives to such a partnership? Could they weather turbulent times?

As the young couple reached a point on the beach where they decided they should turn around and go back, Margaret glanced down and noticed their footprints had been washed away by the tide. Thinking it was an omen, Margaret pointed at the shore and remarked, "Maybe that's what will happen to us. . . . Maybe our dreams are all going to wash away."

Undaunted, Paul replied, "When things are tough for you, I'll help you. And when things are tough for me, you'll help me. We will help each other. That's the way a good marriage works." But as they continued walking, Margaret once again glanced down, this time noticing that only one set of prints had been washed away. Again Margaret was disturbed by what she saw, thinking it didn't bode well for their future. "Well, if our married life is to be like this," she said, pointing out the single set of prints, "we don't stand much of a chance." At this, Paul gently swooped his love up onto his shoulders and carried her along the beach. Finally setting her down, he said, "Margaret, I want to impress upon you that when life gets so bad that it seems there's nothing we can do to help each other, God will carry us." Then, pointing at the single set of footprints the two of them had just created, Paul explained, "Judging from the tracks we just made, you couldn't tell that I carried you, but I did. And that's the way it works with God."

Though he couldn't have known it then, his impassioned repartee would produce a psalm for the whole world. Certainly it did for Margaret, who found Paul's words fortifying and reassuring in relation to the weight of her impending marriage. And it was a wondrous thing to have found Paul, a loving, kind, and good man, and one so committed to the spiritual beliefs they both shared. Here was a man who vowed he would be with her through good times, bad times, all times. She did believe that God would carry them when as a couple they were unable to bear their troubles alone.

But Paul's words carried significance beyond the two of them. As a Christian woman Margaret knew how encompassing God is, and so this promise of support and relief would not only be available to the two of them, but a gift available to anyone: All of us at one time or another experience tough times, heartache, or loneliness; and when we do, we need comforting. While others may reach out to love us and offer us solace, no one can mollify what ails us and replace our heartache with the serenity and strength that a power greater than ourselves can. Like the caretaking arms of a loving earthly father willingly offer solace to his child, the loving and faithful arms of her heavenly Father would reach out to offer *everyone* even more: Through our times of most profound need, any and all of us would be *carried*.

That night, as these thoughts stirred within her, Margaret recalled Paul's words and envisioned their enactment. So moved by this, Margaret got up and, recollecting the words so clearly etched on her heart, placed pen to paper and "Footprints," a piece that is loved the world over—a piece brought about after hours of wrestling with the darkness of doubt and despair—was recorded.

Today, Paul and Margaret continue to work side by side in youth and children's ministries, and they have two grown daughters. Through the years, just as Paul promised, they have helped each other. "Footprints" has stood the test of time and continues to comfort them and so many others during times of struggle—just as it gave Paul comfort while recovering from a heart attack. Even when the original manuscript of "Footprints," packed in a box with other documents, was lost by a moving company when the author and her family relocated across country, the prose refused to be lost to readers in need of its comfort and strength and began to appear printed anonymously. Years later, Margaret Fishback Powers proved that she is the legal and rightful author. Today, "Footprints" is one of the most widely distributed inspirational pieces in print, a treasured pearl worn by millions as they confront their own heavy hearts—and turn their eyes heavenward for comfort during "the very lowest and saddest times" of their lives. Hearing the words, "My precious child, I love you and would never leave you," our hearts are touched by a soul-deep knowledge that we are precious in His sight, and that we are in His sight always. With these words, we know that we are loved and sustained *unconditionally* and are granted the succor of a sense of connection with the greatest caretaker of all.

The omnipotent lustrous pearl of "Footprints" reminds us that we are never, ever, *alone*.

Phantom of New Fine Hall

Give up to grace. The ocean takes care of each wave til it gets to shore.

RUMI

Almost every newcomer to Princeton in the 1970s would come across a peculiar man most especially if their days were spent in New Fine Hall, where most math and physics majors spent their waking hours. Thin, sallow, and sad, the silent man paced the halls night and day, usually dressed in khaki pants, a plaid flannel shirt, and red high-top Keds. A newcomer need only ask any sophomore about the man to learn the Phantom of New Fine Hall was a mathematical genius who had lost his mind. Though no one knew why, The Phantom often wrote mysterious messages on one of the many blackboards that lined the corridors linking Jadwin and New Fine Halls. No one had any idea what many of the messages meant; some seemed nonsensical, while some seemed purely mathematical, others numerological, and still others contained indirect references to past events. For sure, none of the students wanted to meet the same fate as the Phantom, and so whenever anyone grew too caught up in his studies or was said to "lack a social life," other students would warn: "Be careful or you'll end up like the Phantom of New Fine Hall." On the other hand, if a newer student complained about the Phantom's presence, he was immediately silenced with, "He's a better mathematician than you'll ever be!" The newcomer would next be informed that the Phantom had friends in high places at the university and students were not to disturb him. Although this seemed strange, it proved to be true. The Phantom's presence seemed to be not only tolerated but benevolently accepted among Princeton's professors and deans—some of whom, on occasion, even offered the mysterious wraith a friendly greeting as they passed him in the halls—a greeting that almost always remained unacknowledged.

Some feared they would end up like him; some feared they could never measure up to the mathematical brilliance he'd once proved to possess. Such duplicity.

Throughout his life, John Forbes Nash, Jr.—the man referred to as the "The Phantom of New Fine Hall"—had routinely inspired this reaction in others. In part, this accounts for visiting alumni being far more intrigued by the sight of the Phantom than any new student could ever possibly be. His appearance and manner compelled a second look—which brought shocked recognition of him as the brilliant student he had been long ago. Yet even then John Nash had been considered an enigma. While most scholars admired his genius in the field of mathematics, they found his personality unbearable. He was a brazen young man, one who was "full of himself" and thought he had all the answers. If his genius didn't already make him memorable, no one could forget his gall— it was almost legendary on campus.

Tall and handsome, the broad-shouldered first-year student brashly marched into Albert Einstein's Princeton office and requested an audience with the famous physicist. "I have an idea concerning gravity, friction, and radiation, which I'm positive Dr. Einstein would be interested in hearing about," he announced to the physicist's secretary in his typically clipped and condescending tone. The secretary was taken aback by the first-year student's verve and complete lack of humility in asking to meet with the renowned Dr. Einstein— particularly since his words sounded more like an order than a request. Striding into the famed scientist's office, in his usual haughty and aloof manner, the student declared his purpose in being there. Then, without securing an invitation, he went to the blackboard and began scribbling equations and expounding at length on his latest "theory." Listening intently with an open mind (and no doubt also with an awareness of the neophyte's great intelligence and ego), the eminent physicist seriously considered all the young man was proposing. Thirty minutes into the discourse Einstein offered a kindly smile and a gracious word of advice, "You had better study some more physics, young man. And now, you may take your leave."

Of course, the story got around the campus, one more example to be added to the brilliant student's already profile as being arrogant, detached, secretive, and self-absorbed—not to mention cruel and unpredictably angry. Looking down on people who didn't match his IQ or academic standing, John Nash didn't hesitate to call them ignorant, or worse, fools. And he was fond of coaxing others to ask him a question—any question, a complex mathematical equation, great algebraic or statistical riddles, anything at all—just so long as it gave him the opportunity to display *his* superior mind. In other words, John Nash, Jr., was the kind of person others delighted in hearing had experienced such a humbling encounter as the one with Dr. Einstein.

Yet no matter what opinion John's personality elicited, all were forced to agree that John Forbes Nash, Jr., *had been* arguably the most remarkable mathematician of the second half of the century.

The genius of John Forbes Nash, Jr., unfolded early and gained him recognition and respect. While still only in his twenties, his career was in full bloom. He traveled widely and was called upon to lecture before the most eminent of his peers. He ran in a circle of the most elite mathematicians of his day—and was considered by many to be the "best of the best." His intelligence and imagination combined to both entertain and engage in games of mathematical theories and strategies—economic rivalry, computer architecture, the shape of the universe, the geometry of imaginary spaces, the mystery of prime numbers—in ways that dazzled even the best minds of the time. Nash's mathematical insights into the equations of the dynamics of human rivalry—his theory of rational conflict and cooperation—remains one of the most influential ideas of the twentieth century, having transformed the then young science of economics. His scope in the field was broad, ranging from research on algebraic manifolds (which established him as a pure mathematician), to the important work he performed in fluid dynamics. Other great scholars marveled at how Nash just knew exactly which factors out of possible hundreds of thousands were the *most* important.

No one in the world of mathematics would deny Nash had an exceptional mind. Certainly not the RAND Corporation, who recruited the twenty-two-year-old Nash during the years of the Cold War. In the business of "thinking the unthinkable," and under an air force contract to apply rational analysis and the latest quantitative methods to the problem of how to use the terrifying new nuclear weaponry to forestall war with Russia, RAND wanted John on their team. RAND considered his employment with them of utmost importance in furthering their research. This was quite a compliment! RAND attracted only the very best minds in the fields of mathematics, physics, political science, and economics. Selection for work with RAND was an indication that you were the elite—and the brilliant mind of John Nash qualified him for that category.

Then, one day no more than a few years following his work with RAND, like a cruel cosmic joke, the man who produced a compelling theory of rational behavior was no longer rational—nor logical! The sharp gleam of intelligence became a fixed expression. The once handsome, vital man became the hollow-cheeked, sunken-eyed figure who now looked twice his age. Once so determined to impress with his superiority, he now preferred isolation. Confused and delusional, the stellar mathematician aimlessly now wandered the corridors of New Fine Hall.

John Forbes Nash, Jr., suffered from schizophrenia.

First hospitalized for his illness shortly before his thirty-first birthday, John slipped further and further into his delusional thinking, which was a peculiar blend of omnipotence and impotence. Though hospitalized intermittently, for the most part John was cared for by family during his illness. His prolonged, recurring episodes of schizophrenia were to last nearly twenty years.

Yet, slowly, miraculously, John emerged from his schizophrenia.

While he roamed Princeton, a phantom of his former self, it would have been easy for anyone who met or saw him then to write him off as just another mentally ill person, forever lost to the world of reality. Yet, since his remission, John has returned to his work. Most recently he's applying himself to developing a mathematically correct theory of a nonexpanding universe, and he's lecturing once again. He has also regained the admiration of his fellow physicists and mathematicians. Today, Nash's concepts in the area of game theory are considered great basic paradigms in the field of social sciences and biology. So much so that in 1994 John Forbes Nash, Jr., was awarded the Nobel Prize in Economics! He continues to receive recognition—as recently as 1996, he was nominated by colleagues for membership in the National Academy of Sciences.

Not all of his awards are outward signs of achievement. In fact, the one he prizes above all others has been the most hard won. Almost as remarkable as John's miraculous recovery from schizophrenia is the complete metamorphosis of his heart. It's this hard-won transformation that John considers his greatest prize.

Jorgen Weibull was sent to Princeton by the Nobel Prize Committee to meet with Nash and determine if he was rational enough to be considered for the award. In his pressed dress slacks and starched, long-sleeved white shirt, John was polite, quietly articulate, and obviously nervous. Exchanging handshakes and introductions, Weibull led the way towards the entrance of the faculty club, where he planned to interview John. As they reached the door, the once brash young student stopped and questioned, "Can I go in?" then glanced up to meet Weibull's puzzled gaze and explained, "I'm not faculty." Jorgen Weibull's eyes widened as his heart was touched by the man's humility, and the irony of that humility. The formerly arrogant student was now a renowned figure—yet it was now that he knew humility. Questioning whether or not he had the right to eat in the faculty club was quite a departure from the first-year student who had marched into Albert Einstein's office and all but demanded an audience with him.

Unlike the haughty, self-absorbed Nash of the past, today others describe John as unpretentious. The cocky young man who felt superior, infallible, immune, and above ordinary human dictates, now has a different sense of people. Though he was once known to set up cruel pranks and was openly contemptuous—especially if peers didn't meet his intellectual level—now he is a compassionate and kind man, a man whose straight-from-the-heart candor endears him to others. He genuinely cares about and respects other people, as evidenced by those closest to him. Once estranged, he and his wife now rely on each other, and it has been said "he sets his clock by her." He also works conscientiously on showing his two adult sons that he loves them, seeking to make amends for his lack of involvement and care throughout their childhood and youth. The once self-centered man now counts his family and friends among his anchors for a sense of meaning, purpose, direction, and love.

John Nash has triumphed over his mental illness and his self-centered existence. Choosing light, his spirit walked out of the corridors of darkness. The genius returned, surpassing the genius he had previously been.

Certainly the changes in John Nash confound and amaze any who have witnessed them—from a handsome young student who brashly entered the office of a world-famous expert—unannounced and unscheduled—to the sallow specter who drifted in the shadows of academic halls avoiding human interaction, to his sincere demeanor today. Looking at him now, you couldn't possibly know the years of disoriented agony he spent wandering the corridors of New Fine Hall; nor could you know when looking at the Phantom of those days that you were in the presence of a man who would be accepting a Nobel Prize years later. As the old saying goes, "You can't judge a book by its cover."

Knowing so little, if anything, of the past or present transformations that comprise another's life, perhaps it's best to refrain from judging them. After all, each of us is our own pearl in the making—each of us is making our way on the journey of life. The spirit goes where it must go and does the things it must do to accomplish what it must. Perhaps it's enough to honor that we each may travel a different road, each with a different map to follow, a map sometimes not even decipherable to us until we get to each bend in the road.

Certainly we can't always know or understand the detours of another's journey. Nor are we always apprised of what each individual soul uses as fuel on its journey—whatever road it travels.

Author's Note: Schizophrenia is a neurological chemical imbalance, whose symptoms include hearing voices, bizarre delusions, extreme apathy or agitation, and coldness towards others, and can be slightly, moderately, severely, or absolutely disabling. The onset of illness can occur at any time from adolescence to advanced middle age. While the entire course of the disease can be limited to only one or two episodes, more often those afflicted suffer many progressively severe episodes, occurring at ever shorter intervals.

a.k.a. Superman

"Life shrinks or expands in proportion to one's courage."
—ANAÏS NIN

Recently I keynoted a conference in Baltimore, Maryland, and in the question and answer session that followed, I was asked to name several people whom I most admired, those I thought were "modern-day heroes." I listed several and then turned the question back to the group. "What about you?" I asked. "Who do you most admire? Who would you consider 'modern-day heroes'?"

The group tossed out a dozen or so names. At the mention of a particular person's name, you could hear sporadic murmurs of consensus from the others in the group: "Umhmm . . . Mmmhm . . . Yes." But when the name Christopher Reeve was mentioned, the voices rose in unison. The entire room of nearly twelve hundred conference participants unanimously voiced their complete approval, "Absolutely! For sure a hero!"

"Why?" I prodded, wanting them to identify the qualities that made Christopher Reeve stand head and shoulders above the others mentioned. At first the room of corporate leaders and managers said nothing, looking at me suspiciously, weighing the possibility that I might dare not respect and admire our very own modern-day Superman.

Why did the group of conference participants admire and agree so enthusiastically on Christopher Reeve? Is it because of his brave and heroic comeback after such a life-altering accident? As most all the world knows, Christopher—a.k.a. Superman—suffered permanent paralysis when he was thrown from his horse in May of 1995, breaking his first and second cervical vertebra. As a result of the accident, the much-admired television and screen actor, avid skier, and skilled horseman, is dependent upon a ventilator to even breathe.

Most of us were stunned that our handsome young hero—on screen and off—should have such a tragedy befall him. The magnitude of adjustments he'd have to make was staggering: When you've had the kind of dynamic life he lived, how do you adjust to suddenly being confined to a wheelchair? How do you stay optimistic and excited about the future when each day suddenly becomes a set regimen of predictable routines? How do you "ego-adjust" when your public and personal image is of a capable young superman, only now you depend solely on others, no longer able to feed and bathe yourself much less to soar through the clouds on screen or off? In the face of such a turn of events, how does anyone muster up the courage, the will, or even the desire to go on? For anyone to answer such pivotal questions must surely require the rethinking of one's entire life.

For Christopher, in the days immediately following the accident, rethinking his life was as basic as choosing life at all. Candid about his despair during this time, Christopher admits to having thoughts of suicide. "Maybe we should let me go," he said to his wife. "But you are still you," she assured him. He struggled to believe her words, since he didn't feel—nor could he be—like himself at all. "You are my husband, my son's father," she pleaded.

Her words would be his encouragement and motivation to go on.

And so he began, one day at a time, hour by agonizing hour, facing the obstacles. Overwhelming obstacles. Even the "simple" task of getting up each day is a tedious repetition of a scheduled regime, one that takes a full-time staff to carry out. His day begins at 8:00 A.M. when the morning shift arrives. The nurse counts out his twenty pills and vitamins to help control spasms, some to maintain proper functioning of his internal organs. Then, after taking his first round of pills for the day, Christopher begins the very painful process of his stretching exercises. Because his body has been in the same position all night, his joints, muscles, and neck are all stiff. Lasting a full hour, the staff manipulates his body through a strenuous routine of exercises carefully coordinated to make certain every muscle group is worked equally. After this, he is bathed, dressed, and lifted into his chair. From start to finish this whole morning process can take up to three hours. Next, he eats breakfast and then his workday begins. Getting him to bed at night entails a similar schedule. Chris endures a solid five-plus hours of such pain and tedium each day!

Almost anyone can feel sympathy and compassion for Christopher because he endures the rigors of this routine. Yet, many others who find their lives so dramatically changed as the result of an illness, accident, or misfortune, also endure such challenge. While we also "feel for" any such person, we don't usually view them all as heroic.

What is it about Christopher Reeve that so draws our admiration? Maybe we admire how Christopher courageously and optimistically looks forward, instead of feeling sorry for himself or becoming complacent. Without hesitance in his voice he informs us that he intends to walk again. Maybe we admire how he continues to work so diligently on rebuilding his life and how, even with his present disabilities, he's back to being productive—*very* productive. In true Superman style, Chris established the Christopher Reeve Foundation and is a dedicated and ardent spokesman, tirelessly crusading to raise money for the American Paralysis Association. When he isn't traveling to attend speaking engagements or to visit doctors and scientists to learn of progress in research on nerve regeneration and of new discoveries in the field of spinal cord injuries, he's on the phone searching for funding or planning events to raise money for spinal cord injury research.

In addition to lending his celebrity to advancing the field of research and fundraising for those whose lives depend on nothing short of a major modern miracle and scientific breakthrough to reverse what an accident or illness has taken away, he's recreating his career in the motion-picture industry. Less than two years after his accident, he made his directing debut in a made-for-television special, *In the Gloaming*, a movie that was nominated for five Emmys and won four Cable Ace Awards, including Best Dramatic Special. And, he's returned to acting, leading off with a starring role in the television remake of the Hitchcock classic, *Rear Window*. He's also written a book, "Still Me," a candid look at his life, both before and since being in a wheelchair.

It's a fairly comprehensive workload and grueling schedule, even for Superman!

His award-winning professional achievements are nothing short of laudable! Christopher is back winning rave reviews for his work on and off the big screen, and, as the conference audience so enthusiastically expressed, he's *still* winning the public's rave reviews, too. Is it because of his collective phenomenal achievements that the Baltimore audience endorsed him as the poster boy of comeback heroes? Or, is it something more?

Perhaps it's because his personal life as well as his professional life has been lived in the public's eye, and so we feel we *know* him. Year after year, film after film, we've practically watched him grow up. We follow his films, read about him in the tabloids, attune to his interviews. We see photos of him as a social activist, a sports enthusiast, an amiable and social man who loves his family, friends, and fans. We know something of his life—or at least we feel we do. And then, within the tick of a minute, his life changed drastically, dramatically. Understandably, we feel a tender empathy that such a young, active man, whose life was filled with the freedoms of spontaneity, action, and adventure, has had to forgo these liberties. Certainly his longing for those freedoms remains undiminished. "The sensory deprivation is the most painful," he pines, and then provides a heart-wrenching example: "I haven't been able to give my young son a hug since he was two years old."

If the emotional pang created by a loving father being unable to wrap his arms around his little boy isn't persuasive enough, surely our compassion is elicited when he admits that he's envious when he sees friends embrace each other, knowing that he cannot. No longer being able to ski, no longer being able to take Lois Lane out for a spin in the clouds—there are simply so many things our Superman can no longer do. It's difficult to imagine ourselves not being able to reach out and hold our loved ones or to do the things we want to do when we want to do them. And yet, this is his plight. "I long to hold my kids, my wife, my family, and friends," he pines.

Tears cloud our eyes because we so wish he could.

Do we cast our vote for Christopher because we feel a genuine empathy for a man who, like far too many others, has lost so much? Or is it because for all his struggling, he remains unsinkable? That, after all, is the American way, the patriotic spirit our country was built upon. Certainly managers and leaders can identify with an entrepreneurial spirit that believes when something goes awry, it's prudent to assess the losses, regroup, and begin again—as does Christopher: "It's still very difficult to accept the turn my life has taken simply because of one unlucky moment," Christopher concedes slowly, each word heartfelt. "Still, each day takes so much effort."

Perhaps it's his determination and continual effort to pick up the pieces and begin again that endears him to us. We're inspired by how he's coming to terms with his "one unlucky moment" and how he's chosen to transform it, amazed that after such a life-altering tragedy, he has a positive outlook towards doing whatever it takes to go forward. And, we genuinely admire his application of the art of living in the moment—even when it seems so bleak and painful and the past is so seductive. Is it his intelligent tenacity to make meaning of his life and to insist on a meaningful life that grabs our hearts the most?

Certainly any one of these examples is adequate reason why Christopher Reeve is adored and worthy of our admiration. And yet, none of these accounts were among the reasons as to why corporate leaders and managers at the conference that day singled Mr. Reeve out as their first choice of "most admired." What is?

"He's a *giver* rather than *taker!*" they said. "We admire Christopher because he exemplifies a trait that is most honorable and all too rare in today's times: He considers the needs of others."

That he has. "I know I have to give when sometimes I really want to take," Christopher confirms, and then explains it at a level we can all understand—and in a way that goes directly to work on our hearts. "My son is filled with the joy of a five-year-old . . . . If I were to give in to self-pity or express my anger in front of Will, it would place an unfair burden on this carefree five-year-old." Selflessly, Christopher takes to heart that should he allow himself to become bitter and mourn his past too much, he'll isolate and distance himself from his two teenagers, who "need me to be strong and believe that I am capable of knowing what to do when times are tough for them." He is loving enough, secure enough, man enough, to consider what life would be like for his wife should he let himself go and become "a depressed hulk in a wheelchair." He ponders what effect he would have on the lives of other people, most especially his family, if he did anything other than put his best foot forward—even though meeting their needs "takes so much effort." Having contemplated such worthy ideals, Christopher has made the decision to give them the best possible father and husband that he can be.

"A *giver* rather than *taker!*" How refreshing. *Considering the needs of others* is a value we cherish, one so many yearn for a return to within ourselves and within our society. In a time when we have reason to doubt the scruples of leaders because unless or until they are caught, "misleading" the public for self-serving reasons "just happens"; in a time when self-centeredness prevails to such an extent that it's taken for granted; in a time when we are self-absorbed to the point of believing we can look in the mirror, blow ourselves a kiss, and chant "I love myself" and thereby fortify our own self-worth— Christopher reminds us that we live in a world with others, and that in addition to caring for ourselves, we must also think about how our words and deeds affect others.

The emphasis on *interdependence* is a helpful reminder. Thinking of others may be one of the best ways to "find" ourselves and to love ourselves. And, as Christopher found out, it can also be instrumental in helping us recalibrate our needs and goals. Just as "consideration for others" was a key factor in resurrecting his will to live, it was also the grit that reignited his spirit to redirect his life. And, it is because of this—as much as his determination and courage—that his life has become a pearl to the rest us. We are genuinely moved by the essence of Christopher's humanness and consideration for others. Surely given his circumstances following the accident, we were prepared to allow Christopher to be self-absorbed, disillusioned, even angry. Instead, he rebounded in grand style, commanding respect for a comeback filled with phenomenal achievements. No wonder he's gained our respect— and continues to win our hearts.

Just as Superman always rushed to the rescue of those in need in spite of any danger or inconvenience to himself, even in a wheelchair, Christopher Reeve—our own Superman— spins to our rescue in a time of character crisis. The audience in Baltimore saw correctly: Christopher Reeve, his brand of heroism by authentic example of character makes him a modern-day hero. And, a "super man," who can still take flight towards the future!

Full, Flat-Out Passion

The heart is forever inexperienced.
HENRY DAVID THOREAU

On his way from a meeting in San Luis Obispo to a conference in San Diego, thirty-six-year-old Steve Wilkins drove down the scenic coastal highway paralleling the Pacific Ocean, admiring the panorama of the sunset s garnet skies. At the precise moment when the fuchsia sun dropped into the horizon and a sliver of moon winked in the cloudless violet sky, he glanced at his watch and noted that it was 7:15. Spotting a sign indicating that there were pay phones up ahead, Steve decided to exit the freeway to call his wife, Lori. When Lori answered, Steve complained that he was running late. At the rate I m going, I ll be lucky if I arrive in time for the opening keynote, he joked. Knowing he must be exhausted, Lori advised him to stop for the night and get some rest, even if it meant he might arrive at the conference a few hours later than expected. But Steve wanted to press on. He promised to call her when he got to his hotel.

By the time Steve called again, it was well after midnight—but he wasn't calling from his hotel room. His 1996 Lexus had been struck head-on, and Steve was in a hospital emergency room!

Steve had almost reached his destination that fateful night, a military base where he would present his company's computer-based training program during a two-day conference. He was only one mile from the gates of the base and just one mile from his hotel when an intoxicated driver plowed into his car. The thunderous sound of the shattering impact brought the gate guards from the base racing to the scene of the accident. To their great amazement, Steve was not only alive, but coherent.

The doctors that examined him at the hospital concluded that Steve was going to be okay, though they predicted it would take a long time to heal the many muscle and bone bruises, torn ligaments, and overall trauma.

Her eyes widening with each new piece of information, Lori held the receiver to her ear and tried to digest each disturbing detail. Steve had been badly hurt, and the doctors wanted him to fly home as soon as possible before movement became physically unbearable. Hanging up the phone, she immediately took care of the flight arrangements, then went to the kitchen to brew a cup of herbal tea to try and calm herself. Steve had survived a terrifying car crash against great odds— he was lucky to be alive. She knew her husband was going to be fine, but the thought that he could have died scared her. He was the first and only man she had ever loved. . . .

Steve and Lori had been high-school sweethearts. Already certain they wanted to spend the rest of their lives together, they applied to the same universities, agreeing to attend only where both got accepted. Four years later, having graduated from college—both with honors—they looked for work, a requirement that they be able to live in the same city. Now employed and united as ever, they supported each other's professional dreams as they leaped into their individual careers— he as an aspiring writer and computer analyst and she working her way up to a division manager for a large corporation. But no matter how time-consuming their careers became, their lives revolved around each other.

Each other was what gave meaning and purpose to their lives.

A soul mate affair, it was simply a spectacular love—energizing and filled with fun. There were dinners at small candle-lit tables in the back of restaurants where they hardly noticed anyone but each other. On weekends, they watched sunsets in each other's arms and had twilight picnics on the beach. They spent hours cuddling while engaged in intimate conversations, hand-holding, and passionate kisses . . . and planned for exciting trips away alone together, ones they took each and every year. Together they visited among the world's most prized sights and wonders: the Great Wall of China, the Taj Majal, the Aztec ruins. Side by side they enjoyed the splendor of stunning deserts and some of the most beautiful tropical islands—one of which was the Seychelles. It was here in the Seychelles that they spent a glorious week on the Praslin Island, the second largest of the archipelago's ninety-two islands. In the exquisite setting of this island, ringed with great stretches of sand interrupted only by an occasional sun-bleached tree trunk or wind-sculptured rock, they became engaged. They had stayed at the Village du Pecheur, situated

on the beach of the Cote d'Or, a delightful little hotel made up
of five thatch-roofed chalets. During a dinner under the stars,
in a place where oxcarts meet the ferry, where no cars disturb
the tranquillity of the island, and La Passe, the unpaved street
of the village, is swept clean by a woman with a palm-frond
broom, Steve proposed marriage.

In love and absolutely positive they were meant to be
together always, they married, both completely convinced
that their love was eternal and their marriage was destined to
stand the test of time. All this set the tone for how she envisioned their marriage playing out.

But, now, life seemed to be filled with one set of problems
after another.

Lori sat down at the kitchen nook with her tea and wondered how long it had been since she felt as full and in love as
she had in those years. Where had the optimistic, giddy-in-
love woman-child gone—the one who had laughed so freely
and given herself so fully? Where was that girl? Now it
seemed that carefree and happy spirit could scarcely ever be
found—if she could be found *at all*.

There had been so many struggles in their young marriage.
Building a profitable business with a handful of hired help to
over fifty employees in just four years brought with it plenty
of hard work, sleepless nights, and a hefty portion of fiscal and
personnel problems. The pressures of Steve's routine of sev-
enty-five hours a week at the office, not to mention a hectic
travel schedule, left little time and energy for a family, let alone
time for the two of them to spend together as a couple. In fact,
his travel schedule was so heavy that he woefully joked that he
had earned the top rank of practically all of the major airlines'
frequent flyer clubs. Lori shuttled her husband to and from the

airport with dizzying frequency, their small daughter strapped into her infant car seat in the back.

Lori's pace was as hectic as her husband's. Before the birth of their baby, she devoted nearly fifty hours a week to the company and only scaled back to twenty hours a week when the later months of her pregnancy demanded it. Now she juggled flight schedules and baby bottles and picked up the slack at the office. Their lives had changed so much . . . .

What happened to all the intimacy she and Steve had once shared? To all their plans and promises to always travel and treat themselves and each other to the wonders of the world and romantic times together, such as those they had once reveled in and made a priority in their lives? How had all the happiness, joy, true communion, and love between them drained away? Where had love gone? Where had *her* love gone? Why *didn't* she feel what she had once felt for her husband? *When* and, most importantly, *why* had she stopped doing the little things that showed she cared about their romance—like brushing her hair and putting on lipstick and perfume right before he got home? Exactly *when* was it that she stopped calling his office just to hear his voice and to let him know that she loved him? At what point did her calls become centered mostly around household emergencies or dry reports of obligatory contact and mundane directions or requests? "The baby is running a high fever . . . . I won't be home until later than expected . . . . I need you to pick up salad dressing on the way home." Where was any intimacy or romance in those communications? Why did business success, the day-to-day demands of caring for a child, and living daily life get in the way of late-night candles, the scent of freshly dabbed perfume, and the whispering of sweet nothings? Now, with all the pressures and responsibilities of work and marriage, their relationship seemed to be nothing other than a boring routine and a lot of hard work. Was this supposed to be love? For Lori it was beginning to resemble duty and not much more. When had her love died? How long had she been unhappy?

How long had she been contemplating asking Steve for a *divorce?*

And now this. There was no way she could ever fathom leaving Steve at a time as critical and difficult for him as this. Her husband had been in an accident—one so serious he could have been killed. "Yes, but he would be fine," she assured herself once again. Yet if this sense of relief produced a ray of sunshine, it was extinguished by the ominous cloud of how unhappy she felt and shrouded by the fact she wanted out of the marriage. As if an omen, she spotted the notes she had taken just today as she visited with an attorney: Lori was considering filing for divorce.

After checking on her toddler, Lori lay down on the couch, distressed by both her worry about her husband and the tormented discontent she'd been feeling for months of their ailing marriage. She took comfort in the fact that at least their union had borne some fruit. They achieved many of their dreams while still only in their early thirties: they had done a great deal of traveling before the baby was born; they had a thriving business; they had loving family and friends. And they had their precious two-year-old daughter. "So what is your problem, anyway?" she asked herself out loud. But she needn't have spoken the words. Her heart had already "heard" and had already given up an answer. "Okay," she retorted, again aloud. "The passion is gone. And I don't want to live without passion." Correcting herself she said, "*Won't* live without passion. But what am I supposed to do?"

Frustrated, she sipped on her tea and wondered how she could best come to terms with the magnitude of love's greatest loss. How does such an intoxicating romance go from red-hot to being mysteriously snuffed out? Why couldn't she jump-start her passion? And, was it even possible to recapture love? Then, a thought occurred to her: Could the accident in some way help the couple breathe renewed life into what they had lost? Perhaps Steve's accident would slow them both down, give them more time together, and help them appreciate each other. Maybe the accident would be a turning point, a crisis that would trigger change in a love affair that needed rescuing. "Yes!" she resolved, in the early morning hour sitting at the kitchen table. "This is our chance to rekindle love!" With every ounce of resolve, Lori decided that was the new plan. She would use this crisis to "jump-start passion."

It wasn't to be.

With his body so badly bruised and his muscles so battered, Steve's recovery was slow. Once again, Lori worked diligently to fill in for her husband at the office. But with her small baby and injured husband at home, it was all she could do to maintain her sanity, let alone run a thriving business. Steve went back to work as soon as he could, which was much sooner than he should have. In pain—and often skipping physical therapy sessions—Steve jumped back into work like a mad man. Often irritable from his pain, very tired, and under a great deal of pressure, it was hardly a time when Steve was at his best. And, with a precocious and active two-year-old, working long hours at the office and at home, Lori was fairing little better than Steve in the patience department. Then, Lori found out she was pregnant. The couple had always planned on having two children who were close in age, so this was good news. Having another baby would bring new joy and a greater sense of family to their relationship. Lori was excited and hopeful at her pregnancy. But her hopes were dashed when she miscarried within a few weeks. Pregnant three months later, she miscarried once more. The doctor told her to wait several years before trying again.

The months following the accident were simply a traumatic time. The load each was carrying—and the continued growth and success of the couple's business and attendant pressures—took precious time away from a couple with so much on their plates. The result produced a phase of utter separateness. Each felt alone, and in fact, was alone, grieving separately and living more and more in separate worlds where they kept their turmoil to themselves. Each privately resentful of being "alone," the two of them were soon barely talking. Seeing that the time following the accident didn't restore the love between them as she'd so hoped it would, Lori believed that nothing could rescue their lost love. Once again, Lori considered filing for divorce.

Seeking out a respected psychotherapist, Lori sought counseling and was referred to a women's support group. It was there that she met the woman who was to be instrumental in helping her find "flat-out passion." In one of her support group meetings, the group's leader, who had been married for thirty-eight years, wryly commented, "I've fallen out of love with my husband at least thirty times. Luckily, I've fallen in love with him at least thirty-one! Such is the nature of romance in marriage." Lori was struck by her comment and listened with great interest as the counselor explained, "There are many pieces to the puzzle of marriage, pieces with different colors and shapes. One piece is a couple's relationship as parents, another their relationship as financial partners, another as a united duo in family and social settings, or as joint caretakers and providers. If one piece of the puzzle is missing, it doesn't necessarily mean that you can't see the larger image of a beautiful picture and enjoy that scene. In the same way, using the pieces that you do have in your marriage, you can build upon and strengthen those parts that are lacking to create the picture of a full, healthy relationship."

The therapist's comment was a turning point for Lori: The missing piece of passion didn't mean her marriage was loveless. It wasn't all or nothing. There was so much about her marriage that was good, that was workable. She could use all the other good parts to build upon and strengthen her marriage to Steve and to recreate their passion—*her* passion. With the hope offered in those words, she was moved to recommit to her marriage, her new goal being to enjoy the pieces of her marriage that did fit together, and allow them to fuel her quest to set the passion between her and Steve ablaze once again.

It has been over three years since Steve and Lori recommitted to their marriage. During lunch a few months ago, I asked Lori what helped them rekindle their love for one another. Turning her one-month-old son away from the sun, Lori looked up at me and smiled as though she was about to impart a great secret. "I don't believe it would have been possible if we both hadn't trusted God to honor our marriage and return the love that was missing," Lori explained. "For my own part, I prayed that God would renew my love for Steve. I asked for a love that would overflow my heart, sweep me off my feet, and inspire me to break out my lace and perfume!"

"And did God answer your prayers?" I asked.

"Hmm, hmmm—and more!" she laughed, and then added, "But it also took a lot of hard work. I'd say the pain of having lost the passion—a pain that for me was like a never-ending dripping faucet, only it was my heart crying for the loss of what we once had—created the pearl that restored vibrancy to our relationship. That we almost lost our marriage, one we were so sure was heaven sent, got us talking about what we wanted most from our marriage and our lives. We thought we had done that, and like many other couples, we thought our great love was enough to keep our marriage strong. But it wasn't enough. We *hadn't* talked about how we would keep love alive in the face of tough work schedules and the daily demands of family life. So here you are with the person of your dreams, only to find that the life that you dreamed of living together doesn't necessarily guarantee that the love your marriage was based upon will remain as you knew it. And while some people are all too quick to tell you to grow up and give up some of these things, you have to decide if you're willing to do that. Should you have to? I didn't want to give up my passion for Steve and I can tell you, I wasn't all that interested in having it transformed. I'm not trying to be selfish, really, I just want to live my life being in love with my husband. But I had to give up unrealistic notions of 'no compromises' on fairy-tale passion. For example, if Steve offered me a choice between an evening of an intimate dinner at the back table of a restaurant or one cuddled on the couch with the baby between us, I'd choose the baby between us.

"And, I've learned not to be so secretive about my pining — you know, not to just wish for things without expressing my pining in concrete examples. Now I talk clearly and specifically about what I want, and so we're more likely to do something about it. Like I felt our passion was getting lost in the day-to-day, nuts-and-bolts of living, so I told Steve about it. We both agreed we were unwilling to give up love and intimacy, to lose that special bond between us. And based on our experiences, we knew what could extinguish the flames of our love and agreed that we had to come first with each other, before work, before our families — even before our children. Prioritizing our values caused us to simplify our lives quite a bit. We talk about what things like love and passion mean to each of us and ask each other how each of us wants and likes to be loved. It's surprising what you find out. Often, it's the little things that you don't communicate that get you into trouble. For example, Steve thought that he was communicating his love by his devotion to making a good living for our family. I needed *him* and not just a hard-working husband and interpreted his spending long hours at work as not making his family his first priority.

"I learned that it wasn't just me who wanted to keep the romance in our marriage. I wasn't willing to put away the scented candles and lacy lingerie, and Steve didn't want that either. I didn't want him to stop shaving and wearing cologne on weekends to look and smell great for me, like he does when he leaves the house in the mornings to go to work.

"Neither of us wanted to give up 'being in love.' It just happened. Now we constantly work to keep it alive. We each do our part. I remind myself to tell the worker bee she's off duty; I spend less energy on having a neat house, something that was really important to me, and make sure I have enough energy to stay up past 9:00 for a back rub and a long cuddle. And, we go that proverbial extra mile for one another—going out of our way to invest ourselves in our relationship and in each other. When we're the most tired, the most frustrated with each other and life, that's when we give each other the most time, energy, and support.

"I'm so thankful that our marriage survived, so thankful that my heart pined and refused to live without passion in our union. Now Steve and I have a marriage that is everything I thought it could be. That we have it at all is really due to Steve's fateful accident. It was the trauma that forced us to confront my unhappiness. If he hadn't needed me to care for him, I would have simply filed for divorce and I would have gone. I would never have my family or the wonderful marriage—and love affair—we have today."

One of the greatest glories of the human spirit is its craving to love and to be loved. It's tenacious in its quest. Just as the heart knows when to send out Cupid's arrows of love, so it knows when to send out arrows to shoot down the enemies of love, such as unhappiness. How fortunate. What if cupid's messenger of pain refused to deliver his arrows warning us of love's demise—if we didn't hear the words of love songs; never missed those subtle but potent sparks of joy within ourselves created from love; didn't miss the sharing of a spectacular setting sun, the smell of perfume, of slipping into lace, the candle-lit silhouette of our lover? What if we never asked, "What's wrong?" and "How can I fix it?" What if we never grieved the loss of love?

Just as the heart fills its quivers with the attributes that enable us to experience the splendors of love, so the heart pierces us with arrows of unhappiness, as it did for Lori, who didn't want to live without passion in her union. In fact, the very idea of it created within her a grave unhappiness, one that demanded attention and change. In the end, it was transformed into happiness—the pearl of a new and decidedly different realm of passion.

Lucky for us, the heart has a magical ability to ignite within us a lantern of pain to guide us back onto the path of love, a path that takes us home to the people we love and with whom we invest so much.

The Commute

"Where you used to be there is a hole in the world,
which I find myself walking around in the daytime
and falling into at night."

— EDNA ST. VINCENT MILLAY

Divorced, struggling to raise two boys by himself, battling bouts of alcoholism, and deep in depression, Patrick Godfrey saw no sight of future happiness, hope, or love. Things were grim. It would take a small miracle to turn them around.

Looking through old photographs at his mother's house, Patrick came across one of himself hugging Margery Southworth, his high school sweetheart, his first true love. He stared at the photo, mesmerized by nostalgic memories, his heart filled with the warmth of his lingering love for her. He wondered why he hadn't married that girl; she had been the love of his life. When he was with her, everything seemed just right. Certainly times were better then for him than they were now.

Patrick wondered why he hadn't realized how good those times were when he was living them. He regretted that he hadn't appreciated them more deeply—most of all he regretted letting Margery Southworth slip out of his life. If given the chance today, he'd never let them happen again.

His gaze went from her photo to the phone. Maybe he couldn't change the past, but he *could* work on changing the present and the future. Setting the photo album aside, Patrick began calling every Southworth in the phonebook. As he reached the bottom of the list, the luck he'd become accustomed to as of late added yet another notch to his checklist of misfortune. No one he called had ever heard of Margery Southworth.

Maybe he just needed to break the monotony of taking the same route to work all these years and so decided change was in order—or perhaps he was unconsciously obeying some higher summons. Whatever the reason or design, the next day Patrick spontaneously took a different route to work and found himself sitting in morning traffic, waiting at the on-ramp to the highway. Although there was no way for Patrick to know it, fate was about to touch his life. Preoccupied with thoughts of Margery—the love they had shared, who and where she might be today—Patrick was startled from his reverie by the car honking next to him. Looking over at the driver, he was surprised to find the driver staring at him. Then, she lifted her sunglasses, smiled—and waved!

And that's exactly how it happened. There she was, his love of fifteen years prior: Margery Southworth! Astonished, he looked again to be sure it really was her. It was. Elated—and dumbfounded—Patrick broke out in amazed laughter, then put his head down on his steering wheel and cried tears of joy. And then, he renewed his relationship with the girl he never stopped loving!

Was his finding Margery Southworth random coincidence or was fate at work, arranging for the crossing of paths at just the right intersection at just the right moment in time in the lives of these two people? Whatever it was, today, eighteen years later, the two people who found themselves side by side in rush-hour traffic are happily commuting through life *together*! And Patrick Godfrey's suffering in his years without his true love formed a pearl of gratitude and commitment to appreciate the joy of their shared commute.

Cliffs Notes on the Heart

"When soul rises to lips you feel the love you've wanted."
—RUMI

It was their tenth wedding anniversary celebration. Romantically, Paul and Polly talked, laughed, and danced with an incessant closeness. "What a cute couple," the woman standing next to me in the buffet line whispered. "They look absolutely made for each other. They even look alike."

It was true: They did look alike. He just slightly taller than she, both with natural blond hair, fair skin, and sky-blue eyes. I smiled in agreement as the beautiful couple was joined on the dance floor by their four children. The oldest was a handsome, curly blond-haired, nine-year-old boy with an especially reverent and polite demeanor. He was followed by his feisty, flaxen-blond seven-year-old sister. Next came the baby of the family, a tousled, towheaded toddler, looking every bit like Dennis the Menace. Finally, the five-year-old appeared, a serene and happy little dark-haired girl with olive skin and brown eyes—a child so distinctly different from the rest of the family that it was impossible not to notice.

Silently, I watched the woman's reaction to this scene of the whole family gathered together. "Well, they must have adopted that one," she whispered wryly out of the corner of her mouth.

I smiled to myself. "Hmmm," I murmured noncommittally, knowing that there was absolutely more than met the eye here. As I watched the couple dance, I recalled our days in college together when they had met and the idealistic goals and dreams they had for their relationship together. They called themselves partners. The rest of us called them soul mates. They were the kind of couple who personified ideal love—and ideal commitment. Even so, they would face an emotionally charged and heart-wrenching crisis.

With all the passion and dreams with which young lovers begin a new life together, they, too, resolved to always be close and united in all things. As it is with most, when their first child was born, it was a time of celebration and adjustments. From all outward appearances, they seemed to manage very well. The birth of their second child added yet more adjustments, and again they met the impending challenges. They seemed happy and close.

Two years later, Polly gave birth to her third child—a little girl noticeably different in appearance from the couple's other children. Paul was not the baby's father.

As one might expect, a transgression of this magnitude is difficult—if not impossible—for any couple to overcome. Polly's four-week affair with a colleague—however brief—

most certainly disturbed the equilibrium of her marriage. The future of this couple's marriage—and family—was at a cross-roads. Would they, could they, remain together? Could they work through the issues that this breach of their vows and their trust in each other brought to the fore?

I had been a part of Paul's support system when he was sorting it all out.

"What an ordeal that was!" he remarked when we talked. "It was rough, really rough, but you know, though I'd never ask to go through it again, it was a lesson more valuable than any I could ever have imagined."

"A lesson?" I asked, wondering how he'd boiled it down to a learning experience. "What was the lesson?"

Looking at me, he recited earnestly, "Take good notes." Then he grinned and asked, "Do you remember whose line that was?"

"Of course I do! Mr. Kappan—Literature 300!" I answered, fondly recalling our college days together.

"That's right! It was Kappan's class," he confirmed, slap-ping my arm playfully.

The memory came rushing back. "Wow, did you ever take so many notes in all your life?"

"Well, his philosophy was that if we took good notes in class, we wouldn't have to study for the test. But after seem-ingly hundreds of pages of notes, rereading them in prepara-tion for the test took about as much time as reading the assigned book which, of course, we never did. Or at least I didn't."

"So instead, we'd head to the bookstore and buy Cliffs Notes!"

"Yup," he agreed. "So that we could get right to the point—to the heart of the matter."

Remembering how very difficult this period in his life was for him, I tried to help him summarize the events, "Cliffs Notes on the heart?"

Looking pensive, my friend nodded and answered, "I needed to sort through the mirage of emotions, all the sub-plots, and get to the core—the bottom line—to find out what really mattered."

"That had to take some serious soul-searching," I commented, really feeling for him.

"That's for sure," he said and then explained, "For me, there were so many different emotions to sort out. I kept hearing different voices—each one equipped with its own loudspeaker—debating with the other about what I should do. It was pure chaos. I couldn't sleep. I couldn't eat."

"Voices? Sounds fairly schizophrenic to me!" I teased.

"Maybe so," he laughed. "Who knows just exactly how crazy we get when dealing with a partner's infidelity!"

"The voices?" I prompted, taking note how Paul often referred to his wife as his partner.

"There was my head talking, my heart talking, and the other voice, let's just call it my 'macho' side, talking," he replied, now able to articulate it. His blue eyes didn't flinch as he met my eyes with calm assurance, admitting, "At first the voices were all garbled. While one wailed in pain and grief and wanted to be held by my wife—wanting reassurance that all would be well—another screamed in resentful accusation, wanting revenge. Each of the voices wanted me to deal with the situation differently.

"My macho voice—my ego—roared the loudest. It reeled with accusations: How could she do this to me? To us? It wanted me to leave her because she betrayed me and the kids. This voice kept saying things like, 'She's made her bed, now let her sleep in it!' I was eaten up with indignation, thinking, I'd never do anything like this to her! And I was embarrassed. I wondered, How many other people know about this? What shall I tell them if they ask? What are they thinking about me now? And then there was the other guy. What did he look like? What did she need from him that I didn't have? This voice produced some pretty rough times, and I realized that if I let the macho voice have its way, it would wreak havoc, playing on all my insecurities to a point where my self-pity and bitter pride would have taken me away from everything I love and want—my family.

"My ego saw everything—from my wife's transgression to my own course of action in response to it—as a matter of black and white. The second voice knew that things weren't that clear-cut. Thoughts from the voice I call my head were more analytical and more rational. It directed me to be reflective and exercise caution before taking any action, to ask questions like, Am I willing to lose my family? What is best for the kids? Can my relationship with my wife be repaired, and if so, what can we do now to fix it and move on?"

"I feel for you," I commented sympathetically, imagining his turmoil in being inundated with such poignant questions while in the midst of emotional crisis. "How did you sort them out?"

"I took a long, hard look at our marriage and inventoried all the pros and cons of staying together," Paul responded. "I looked at the fact that she's a wonderful mother to our children and, in spite of her affair, she's been a loving wife to me, too. And the marriage goes beyond the house and home we live in—although losing that would be tough, too. My parents love her, as do my brothers and sisters. Plus, we've built a life in the community together. Did I want to throw all this away? We'd struggled together to accomplish goals that were important to the both of us.

"And I thought of the possibility of being alone. If I left the marriage, then what? Sunsets alone? Or do I find someone else and start all over again? I'd have this home and that home, kids there, and, if I remarried, maybe kids here. I have men friends who have started all over again. Behind closed doors they'll admit it really isn't the solution." Growing reflective, Paul speculated, "Maybe that's what's wrong today. People just leave, breaking up a family, but that turns out to be tougher than fixing what went wrong."

"Paul, it's admirable that you were able to honestly look at what price your actions would cost, most especially to others," I commented. "How selfless."

Paul thought about my comment and then said, "I had to consider how my actions would ripple to others in the family—regardless of my feelings. I'm happy that I did. Caring about the needs of my kids and parents amplified the loudspeaker from the voice of my heart."

"The third voice?" I inquired. "Yes," Paul verified. "The voice in my heart was a very compassionate one reminding me that we're all human and sometimes frail. It advised me not to feel 'holier than thou' because she had breached our vows and I hadn't. What I liked best about this voice was that it didn't make me run around in circles. It zeroed in on the fact that I loved my wife and my children and didn't want to live apart from them. And it reminded me that what I truly wanted was the closeness and unity my wife and I once had. Cutting through all the emotional upheavals was helpful because, first of all, it didn't take up the energy that being scattered and crazy did, so I could focus my energy on working towards specific goals.

"The real breakthrough came when the reasoned voice of my head joined with the passionate voice of my heart. Combined, this voice asked me to evaluate my leadership role in my family—one in which I always prided myself in doing a good job. Needless to say, I had to reconsider my contributions to each family member. This time, the focus had to extend beyond paying the bills to making their lives better in other ways, beginning with my commitment to my wife.

"This voice also asked me to question what I believed about love. Did my love for my wife mean I love her only as long as she meets my criteria? Did it mean that I love her if she behaves the way I expect her to behave? Did I love her when she loves me the way I want her to love me? This led to 'Is it entirely her fault? Is there something missing in our relationship that made us susceptible to this?' If I'm honest, I have to admit that for more than a year before the affair I'd grown detached."

"But you were so close," I said, remembering what soul mates they were.

"It's easier than you think to misalign your priorities," Paul responded. "For me, that included everything from spending too much time at work to not taking a more active role in my children's day-to-day care." His eyes pinned mine and he continued, "Again, I'm not making excuses for her—or for me, for that matter. Taking responsibility for my part in this equation was difficult and at the same time therapeutic. It was the beginning of my forgiving her and also my asking her to forgive me for neglecting our relationship—all of which contributed to the walls and the distance that grew between us."

"Forgiveness is no small feat," I remarked. "And when we can't forgive ourselves, we stray from the path of being able to forgive others."

"That's for sure," he concurred heartily. "I desperately wanted to forgive my wife. I just didn't know if I could. I didn't know what to do to lessen the feelings I had of bitterness and hurt and the deep sorrow I felt for the loss of the innocence of our love. Yet, I knew I needed to forgive. For one thing, I needed the personal freedom, the peace of mind. And I really did want to be at peace with her, too. Even so, though I knew what I ought to do, I didn't know how. I felt so deeply wronged and offended. It set up a deep internal conflict between what I knew was best and what I felt. But my heart kept prodding, 'You love her and you know she loves you. You can both get through this. Your family is worth the effort.' And I'd yell back, 'How?' And my heart would repeat this impassioned plea, 'Forgive her!' "

"Talking Cliffs Notes!" I teased.

"It sure seemed that way!" Paul replied, now laughing. "So, then I was faced with a choice: Was I willing to work with my feelings, honoring them while directing them? Or, did I want to continue wallowing in the pain and the misery of my bitterness, being directed by my erratic emotions? For me, it was a crisis of the will. I had to be able to deal with me, to manage my feelings. If I wanted to move beyond this and reclaim my family, I had work to do—the process of getting what I wanted started with a conscious decision. I needed to focus on me."

Forgiveness was the silver lining to the cloud of being hurt. In choosing to forgive, Paul triumphed over the agony of feeling betrayed. The result was a deeper level of compassion and understanding of how to love.

"I respect and admire the depth of both your introspection and apparent application of a resolution to your crisis, Paul," I said. "You really worked at this."

"Yes," he responded resolutely. "It was largely the voice of my heart that allowed me to let go and forgive. And steered me towards where I am today—back together with my wife, both of us honestly working towards being happy and secure together. It's a whole renewed sense of commitment."

"Still," I prodded, "forgiving is not the same as forgetting. How did you forget?"

"I choose not to call to mind the hurt," he replied succinctly.

"Is that really possible?" I asked, wondering if he had reduced forgetting to "distraction."

"I choose not to dwell on the past or to obsess about what's been done," he answered. "The more you rehearse a memory, the harder it is to let go of it. I choose to focus on my children, all of them." Looking at the photo sitting on his desk of his children, Paul pointed at the beautiful little child bubbling with smiles, sitting amid her siblings. "Every day I see this beautiful child and every day I experience her love, so every day there is a renewal of the decision to forgive. It gets easier and easier with time."

"And the other guy?" I asked, knowing I was treading in delicate territory.

"Oh," Paul answered kindly, "whenever I find myself caught in a web of jealousy or revenge or spiteful feelings, I remind myself of my choice to put it away. It's a sincere effort. I didn't just 'stuff it' as the psychologists say, nor am I in denial. I've simply changed the way I view it." Paul grew thoughtful and then added, "For all of us, our lives have a story to tell. In my life, the affair happened. It's a part of my story, but it doesn't have to be the theme. I've reduced it to a subplot."

"So," I said, "the Cliffs Notes to the story of your heart read: 'And then a little girl came along . . . . ' "

Finishing the sentence without prompting, Paul added, "Renewing Paul and Polly's commitment to their marriage, to revamping their short- and long-term goals, and to co-parenting—lovingly, while united under one roof—four very happy and spirited children."

"The end?" I asked.

His eyes softened as they went to a photograph of his wife. "No," he said gently. "Just as Paul's own heart was healed, so was his relationship with his soul mate and life partner—the love of his life. Knowing such love is well worth the price of forgiveness." His eyes moved once again to find the photograph of his four children. He surveyed each of them, then focused on the face of the dark-haired one among them. "And a little girl by the name of Joy came along—a little girl who is a complete joy—and helped teach his heart how to take good notes, in love and in life." His entire face smiling, Paul added, "And because of it, they all live happily ever after." He paused and then asked, "See this smile? I can literally feel it. I love her very much. She is my daughter and a symbol of our family's strength."

The next day, I watched as he gently lifted the small five-year-old out of the passenger side of the family van. While in midair, she wrapped her little arms around him, buried her head in his neck, then grinned up at him and crushed an enthusiastic kiss on his cheek. He chuckled, hugged her tighter, and set her on the ground.

The contrast was striking: He was such a muscular man, and she was such a delicate little girl. He was so fair, blond, and blue-eyed; she was so honey-skinned, dark-haired, and brown-eyed. These surface differences aside, their love for each other was readily apparent. Hand in hand, father and daughter walked to the back of the van, where she held up two little arms, wanting to help him carry the groceries to the house. He opened the van's door and carefully placed a five-pound bag of oranges in her waiting arms.

"Oooh, Daddy!" the little girl squealed, her eyes widening, her small oval face animated. "These are so heeaavy!"

He tossed his head back, erupting in delighted laughter. "Yes, they are, honey, but you are big and strong and can carry them," he said, bolstering her self-confidence by adding, "Can't you!"

Her giggles bursting to be turned loose, she replied emphatically, "I can, Daddy!" Reassuring her sense of ability, he remarked, "I know you can!" Together they walked towards the house—with no break in either the small child's chatter or the man's rapt attention, their mutual adoration apparent in each of their faces.

Watching this touching scene between father and daughter, I felt the warm reassurance of his happiness.

Motivated by love and formed by the work of forgiveness, healing was made possible in Paul's marriage and created the pearl of an ever-deepening commitment to an even greater love.

Poster Boy of Thrill-Seeking

"Whoever can see through all fear will always be safe."
—TAO TE CHING

Montreat, North Carolina, was a small southern town where everyone knew one another. Certainly everyone knew and respected the Reverend Billy Graham and his wife, Ruth. And just as certainly everyone agreed that their son, seventeen-year-old Franklin Graham, was one of the town's rowdiest citizens. But, perhaps out of respect, no one said anything to his parents when Franklin drove his motorcycle and car on the streets of Montreat long before he had a license or complained when he drove fast and recklessly. Perhaps that's why Franklin felt he could get away with just about anything. Perhaps that explains why with each passing year he seemed to grow even more bold, upgrading his antics to include drinking and brawling.

Or, perhaps it was just his nature.

Nurture or nature, he was simply the "town's bad boy," a term he not only earned, but coveted. Pure and simple: Franklin was on a quest for excitement. He made no bones about the kick he got from purposely speeding by Pete, one of Montreat's policemen, who drove a vehicle Franklin mocked as being "ready to be retired." The teen was quite certain that his own car, which he worked on every weekend, could outrun the friendly and patient officer's old junker. Besides, Pete never even bothered to try to catch him. That is, until one particular beautiful spring day in June, when Franklin floored his old, green Triumph Spitfire and zoomed by Pete at nearly ninety miles per hour.

It was one time too many.

Imagine the lanky youth's surprise when he saw the red flashing light in his rearview mirror! Though the law officer's siren was wailing, instead of pulling over, Franklin just raced towards home with the speed of a bullet—and a joy he could hardly contain. Careening into the driveway and howling with glee, he sped up the family's mountain road, watching in his rearview mirror as the gate closed behind him, shutting Pete out. His heart merrily pounding at a rate as accelerated as his driving, Franklin screeched to a halt in front of the house, ran to his room, and kicked the bedroom door closed. Plopping down on his bed, he raked his dark hair back off his forehead, his pulse still dancing as he thought of how he had seen this kind of chase on television. Outfoxing an officer was even more thrilling in real life! Chuckling, he envisioned a freeze frame of the look on Pete's face as he was forced to squeal to a stop in front of the locked gate. "Hah!" the teenager said out loud. "Gotcha, old boy!"

His elation didn't last long.

"Come here, Franklin," his father calmly called from the bottom of the stairs. "Pete just rang. Meet me in the study." Obeying his father, Franklin buttoned his shirt higher at the throat, hitched up his pants, and went downstairs. Attempting a look of casual curiosity, he consciously relaxed the shoulders of his tall frame, looked up innocently, and then asked non-chalantly, "What's up?" He wasn't about to volunteer any-thing incriminating. Such was his style.

"You tell me," his father answered.

Franklin was unable to disguise the fact that he found a great deal of humor in what had just transpired. But his father didn't laugh. In fact, he didn't even smile. "Pete's on his way up," Franklin was informed. "You and I are going to have a meeting with him." His father's expression remained intent and anything but amused—it wasn't the first time young Franklin had recklessly disregarded the values his parents tried to instill in their son. "If he wants to arrest you," his father said, once again at wit's end, "I'm going to support him." With these words, he gave young Franklin a grave look of disappointment and walked away, leaving Franklin alone in the impressive study of wall-to-wall books to think about the consequences of his actions.

Franklin was sorry—not for what he had done, but rather, for getting caught!

Franklin was, as his mother describes him, "as good as he could be and bad as he could get away with." He was, quite simply, a perennial poster boy of thrill-seeking, one who found rebellion worth all its consequences. Preferring instead to do the opposite of whatever was expected of him and taking pride in his individuality, regardless of the situation, Franklin stretched the rules as far as he could and then some.

By the time he was seventeen, young Graham had been smoking and drinking for years, was frequently in brawls, and on numerous occasions suspended from school for fighting. The lad didn't see these consequences of his behavior as a bad thing; they were proof that he was having a good time. They were incidents that made life exciting! There seemed to be no way to persuade the adolescent there were better, more productive—and appropriate—ways to find adventure and excitement in life. He was just being himself, following his nature.

You can only imagine the consternation he caused his parents. And, so, they packed him up and sent him off to a private boys' boarding school. There he was sure to recognize the folly of his ways and reform himself. Besides, his parents reasoned, the structure and individual attention would be good for him. Yes, a private boarding school was the answer.

This proved to be wishful thinking.

Franklin despised the boarding school, but not because the pillows weren't soft enough or the food wasn't tasty enough. No, Franklin's beef with the school was that it had so many *rules*—and Franklin being Franklin, rules simply went against his nature. To Franklin, rules were hypocritical, unjust, or just plain irrelevant. Defiantly, he vowed not to be "broken or brainwashed," to conform to anyone's rules—most especially the school's, which he saw as enemy territory.

Nothing, it appeared, was able to make him surrender his perpetual quest for mutiny!

Facing the inevitability of their son's expulsion, his parents agreed to let Franklin come home to finish high school. Luckily, the rowdy teen managed to graduate from high school—albeit not without incident.

To his parents' even greater relief, Franklin decided to go on to college. But even getting a little older, Franklin didn't outgrow his needs for revolt and insurrection. And so it would take more than the halls of one institution of higher education before he was finally permitted to stay long enough to earn a degree! Franklin was hell-bent on remaining steadfast on his course of constant search for adventurous causes.

He enjoyed these college years. To his pleasure, he found adventure after adventure.

Little did Franklin know, he was about to meet his match.

After completing his freshman year in college, a friend of the family offered Franklin a summer job with a travel agency, which included leading four tours through the Middle East. Action, excitement, uncharted territory—just what Franklin longed for. He jumped at the opportunity.

While on tour, he met and befriended two women—Dr. Eleanor Soltau, an American, and Aileen Coleman, an Australian nurse—who ran the Annoor Sanitarium, a missionary hospital in Mafraq, Jordan, that specialized in treating tuberculosis among the Bedouin people. Nomadic tribal people, the Bedouin lived in tents in the deserts where the harsh elements and weather conditions made them susceptible to tuberculosis. An estimated forty thousand people in Jordan had been infected with the disease, yet there were less than one hundred hospital beds throughout the entire country available for the sick. The inequity in those statistics instantly alerted Franklin's "cause-seeking" senses—as did Eleanor and Aileen's plans to build a new hospital. Franklin was impressed by the courage of these two brave women missionaries. In the middle of the male-dominated Middle Eastern world, women didn't have the same rights as men, yet the gutsy duo rebelled against any thought of being limited by such cultural constraints. Day by day they went about their business, effectively saving lives.

The more Franklin watched these gracious, plucky women successfully carry out their invaluable work, the more intrigued he became. Though their supplies were minimal, Eleanor and Aileen remained undaunted. It seemed nothing fazed them, not even that the hospital had just one beat-up car, a fact that endlessly irked Franklin (PLO guerrilla soldiers had stolen and destroyed their two newer, more reliable vehicles during an uprising against King Hussein about two years earlier). It just didn't seem right that these women would have to make due with such a "hunk of junk"—especially when it might even be called upon to perform as life-saving transportation. After examining their old car, Franklin decided what they should really have was a Land Rover fully equipped for desert usage. This thought sparked a scheme: He would get one and deliver it to them himself, which would also mean that the clever college student would miss his first semester of his sophomore year.

Franklin knew he'd need help and developed a course of action to enlist his father's assistance to raise the money to secure a vehicle for the missionaries. Being a minister, his father's heart was always sensitive to the needs of missionaries. In addition, his organization offered financial support to meet those kinds of needs. A perfect plan!

When Franklin first approached his father with his plan, the minister was understandably a bit skeptical of his son's sudden interest in supporting the causes of missionaries. Nonetheless, his father helped him secure a Land Rover and gave Franklin permission to pick up the vehicle in England, take it across the English Channel by ferry to France, and into Jordan.

Franklin was ecstatic—such a voyage provided him with the adventure he craved, while freeing him from the humdrum academic grind.

After Franklin delivered the Land Rover, he stayed on in Jordan for several months helping the missionaries with the construction of their new hospital. While there, he witnessed firsthand how they turned over challenges to God in prayer— whether rain for the barley crops or funds for medical or building supplies. In their absolute belief that their prayers would be answered, the missionaries seemed to wage a type of open rebellion against all appearance to the contrary. This appealed to Franklin's sense of defiance, and he was continually amazed at how those needs were always met; two things that gave the young man, who had based his life on the firm conviction that he wasn't ever about to surrender, something new to contemplate. To his added surprise, he also discovered that he loved doing work that helped people in need, those who could use a little luck in the form of someone who could tip the rules in their favor. To this end, Franklin, of course, was a master!

Divine providence works in unexpected ways: Perhaps God had a plan for Franklin that required a rebellious and just spirit and had been molding him all along. Though Franklin didn't know it at the time, his excitement when it came to taking on a challenge would lead him to fighting to make the lives of others better. These tasks felt good to him, familiar to him, appeased him—like beating the odds in an impromptu (and less than legal) car race against a newer sports car. The positive effect on the people and their lives was a great source of satisfaction to Franklin.

While doing this work on his own terms and in his own time was just fine with Franklin, he still wasn't about to surrender to anything less than doing everything his way. So when his satisfaction turned on him, growing into the voice of a calling that constantly beckoned and nagged at him, Franklin fought it just as hard as he'd fought against anything that tried to dictate what he should do throughout his youth. He refused to give up his own rules for living—partying and playing just as he wanted, and helping out when and where he decided—expecting even God to accept things on his terms. But Franklin soon learned he could fight, but he couldn't win. He could run, but he couldn't hide. The voice of the calling tormented him with its ever-present insistence.

As the voice continued to nag and coerce, Franklin wrestled with his own mulish desire to have fun. It took him a few years to realize that fun wasn't fun anymore—not while being constantly haunted by his conscience coaxing him to surrender to a greater calling. Finally, Franklin threw up his hands, opened his heart, and decided to make that calling a part of his life.

Three years after his return from Jordan, Franklin made the decision to dedicate his life to Christ and began work with Samaritan's Purse, a Christian relief and evangelism organization that helps victims of war, famine, disease, and natural disasters the world over.

His position with Samaritan's Purse would shape his life and become the altar of his pearl of service to God and others.

The misguided willful rebellion of his youth has been exchanged for one that many people would say is "divinely directed"—a rebellion with a great cause. After all, where there is rebellion there is strength and energy. Who better than Franklin to lead the fight to make certain the needs of victims are met? Striving to achieve the spiritual and physical good of others, Franklin's spirit allows him to fight for what he knows is right and fair and to stand a courageous rebel-warrior for compassion and righteousness.

The youth who once questioned the rules is a man who still questions those he sees as arbitrary or unjust. Once bent on finding a way around rules that didn't suit his purpose, he still finds a way around them—only now his purpose is for the greater good of humanity. For example, during the days of Desert Shield, the American military in Saudi Arabia were not allowed to acknowledge their Christian faith. Mandatorily given literature teaching the Islamic faith as part of a cultural awareness campaign, many Christian American soldiers wanted literature that also explained their faith to share with their Islamic counterparts. Franklin saw no reason why they shouldn't have this opportunity and devised a strategy to see that they could. He urged the crowds he spoke to in America to send tens of thousands of letters of encouragement to American servicemen in Saudi Arabia, letters that were to include Christian literature in Arabic, which Samaritan's Purse provided. Franklin realized that Saudi officials would never be able to censor the volume of mail generated by the letter drive. A few months later, his organization also sent holiday packages to U.S. troops; each included a New Testament in Arabic, a clever plan that was devised to "spread the gospel around the world!"

All this he did even though he knew his efforts weren't welcomed by some—in fact, an army chaplain called to let him know his tactics weren't *at all* appreciated and the U.S. Postal Inspector telephoned him to inform him that sending "religious, alcoholic, and pornographic material" was breaking the law. But leave it to Franklin to find a way around it, and he did. Once again Samaritan's Purse had succeeded in its mission to "minister."

Whether seeing to it that American soldiers in Saudi Arabia received contraband Christian literature during the days of Desert Shield or helping chaplains for the Contra Army in the jungles of Central America in the days of the Sandinistas, Franklin has continued to embrace greater—if sometimes rebellious—causes. Possessed of few qualms in defying arbitrary rules when it comes to achieving goals for a greater cause, Franklin's rebel heart believes in fighting to find a way around them—especially when finding a way around them can save lives, which it often does.

During the tribal war in Rwanda that resulted in the massacre of more than a million people, the passionate humanitarian proved he was more than willing to rebel against any bureaucratic red tape that could cost people their lives. Samaritan's Purse sent a team of doctors and nurses, as well as medical supplies, to aid the victims of that war. Yet the United Nations, because of the inherent danger it posed, refused to allow the medical team to enter Tanzania, where millions of Rwanda's refugees were camped. Sparked ablaze by this injustice, Franklin's rebellion once again ignited a creative solution. Defiantly, he led his team into Uganda, where they drove down to the Rwanda border and found a way to cross over into that country, traveling directly behind the Rwandan Patriotic Front—the rebel army lines.

The redirected rebel succeeded—as he has so many times before and since.

The foundation of Franklin's passion is a spirit of the heart that leads one into battle with more attention on the goal to be accomplished than the fear of consequences; such passion fuels the courageous to achieve purpose. Today, as president of Samaritan's Purse, Franklin travels the world over locating and aiding those who need assistance. He also serves as chairman of the board of World Medical Mission, the medical arm of Samaritan's Purse, which provides mission hospitals with volunteer medical personnel, equipment, training, and financial assistance. And of course, he is an ordained Christian minister and successor to perhaps the greatest evangelical ministry in the world—that of his father, Billy Graham.

Things haven't really changed all that much for the playful maverick who sat listening to Officer Pete that night so many years ago, devising his next strategy to find a loophole, with even the tiniest big enough for him to get through. As children we test the boundaries that are set for us, and as adults we test the limitations with which we have encumbered ourselves. Except for those set by God, Franklin seems to know neither—a trait that serves him well. Having experienced the passion of his youthful rebellion, Franklin knows the thrill of fighting zealously for a cause—even when the odds are stacked against victory or the cause looks most unpopular.

Perhaps it was his own stubborn rebellion that caused his pain as he fought the ever-present calling that haunted him. Ultimately, he learned the value, time, and place for surrender and the pearl of service was formed. Since then, Franklin's spirit of rebellion has created what could be referred to as Samaritan's Purse full of pearls. For today, his very nature, the rebel he fine-tuned in his youth, has become a leader to thousands of souls all over the world as he fights for worthy causes, regardless of the risk. . . . Or maybe because there is risk!

An Exception to the Rules

"Love is what you've been through with somebody."
—JAMES THURBER

Recently my mother was taken by ambulance to the hospital. At first the doctors thought she might have suffered a mild heart attack and so she was immediately placed in the intensive care unit. The doctors suggested my father spend the night at the hospital. Suddenly having the new awareness that he could actually lose her, my father certainly wasn't about to leave her! He stayed.

At the end of the second day, the doctors ruled out a heart attack, but ordered more tests in order to make an accurate diagnosis. Because her condition was still grave, once again the doctors advised my father to spend the night at the hospital. Once again, wrestling with the fear of realizing their time together might some day end, he was not about to have it any other way.

When the tests came back the following day, the doctors confirmed that my mother had experienced a series of mini-strokes. With rest and care she would fully recover. This good news coincided with my mother's improvement in physical and emotional well-being. She was beginning to feel so much better that on the fourth day she was moved from intensive care into a private hospital room. Later that day, once she was resting comfortably, my father told Mom that he was going home to check on things and would return later in the evening during normal visiting hours, which he did.

My father is eighty, and my mother is seventy-three. Perhaps that's why the hospital staff seemed not to "notice" that late that night my father was still there long past the normal visiting hours. And, perhaps the doctor making his rounds early the next morning knew my father had spent the night at the hospital. If he did, he didn't say anything about it to my father that morning. But later that same day, as he completed his rounds, the doctor made a special point of telling my father that his wife would be in good hands, and it would be just fine for him to go home and return when normal visiting hours began the next day. My father kissed my mother good night, and, as suggested, left her room, complying with the rules.

What happened next isn't entirely clear, though as he tells it, he was feeling a bit tired and so he sat down in a chair just inside the laundry closet—you know, to rest for a while. Perhaps he didn't "rest" long enough. Or, more probable, my mother's husband of fifty-plus years had a change of heart and decided to stay with his sweetheart no matter what anyone else advised! This recent scare reinforced what he had always known—they belonged together. Perhaps there's the chance that my father had intentions of leaving the hospital—but he didn't. Instead of finding himself at his car, he found himself back in his wife's room. And you know what? Not a single member of the ample and extensive staff saw him until the nurse on the night shift came into my mother's room around midnight to check on her.

The nurse was quite surprised to find my father fast asleep in the chair beside his wife. "Mr. Burres, you really must go home. Visiting hours are over," she chided. Then she politely reassured him, "Your wife is going to be fine now. We'll call you if her condition changes."

"Oh," my father fretted aloud, pausing momentarily to try and plot a solution, "are there no exceptions to the rules? I mean, it just seems that I should be here. We've been together for fifty-four years . . . . It just doesn't seem right to leave her side when she needs me." He met the nurse's eyes directly.

"I know," the nurse, obviously touched by his sincerity and devotion, replied sympathetically. "Even so, those are the rules." Leaving the room, she added, "I'm sorry, but you must leave." She assumed he did.

But when the nurse checked in on my mother again at around 3:00 A.M., there in the room with her was my father, sound asleep in the chair beside his darling, holding her hand. "Looks like you fell asleep, Mr. Burres," the nurse remarked, patting my father on the shoulders to rouse him. "I'm sorry to have to ask you to leave so late, but you must go."

This time my father tried a different approach. "Oh," he began, "it's such a long way home, and the roads are very icy . . . . "

"Yes, well in that case, you might want to consider getting a room at the hotel the hospital operates as a courtesy to the family members of patients," she advised. "It's right across the street, and the rooms are very reasonable, only nineteen ninety-nine per night." Before she could finish her sentence, my father opened his wallet and took out a twenty-dollar bill. Handing the money to the nurse, he asked, "Could you please take care of paying that for me?" My father insisted the nurse take the twenty dollars. Perhaps not knowing what else to do, the nurse smiled as she shook her head and took the money. Then, after checking that my mother was resting comfortably, she left the room.

The next morning, the doctor entered my mother's room and saw my father and mother holding hands, engaged in lively chatter. "You're here quite early this morning, Mr. Burres," the doctor commented. "I understand you stayed at the hotel. Did you get a good night's sleep?" Not allowing himself to be led into the doctor's trap of having to reveal where he'd spent the night, my father responded, "Nineteen ninety-nine is pretty reasonable for a room, don't you think? And yes, I slept as well as could be expected."

Outfoxed, the silver-haired senior member of the medical staff relented. "Yes, well, it's probably not as comfortable as sleeping in your own chair!" Having said this, the doctor handed my father the twenty dollars the nurse had given him and said, "I hope my wife and I have as long and loving a marriage as you and your wife and that we are as committed to helping each other through those times when we need each other the most. Seems that in your case spending time with your wife has been beneficial—now the both of you can go home."

Perhaps the experienced healer understood what my father now knew more clearly: *Time* with a loved one is not only precious, but therapeutic.

Perhaps the doctor was versed in affairs of the heart as well, and knew that while our souls yearn to "be free" to soar, it's also the spirit's nature to allow itself to be bound. Having found its soul mate—a union with a code of its own—the spirit will honor above all else the rules and regulations of its love. Such has been the nature of my father's love for my mother, his wife all their married life. Yet, even though a devoted soul mate, my father's alarm at losing her created within his heart a pearl of a new rule of its love: She was even more priceless to him than he'd ever imagined and he was bound to live with the knowledge that each and every second together counts.

A Safer Haven

"It is such a secret place, the land of tears."
—ANTOINE DE SAINT-EXUPÉRY

Yet another unsuccessful business meeting punctuated a series of recent setbacks in Burt Medlin's business. Over lunch this afternoon, his most important client threatened to take his business elsewhere if the services Burt's company provided weren't improved within thirty days. Burt spent the remainder of the day working out strategies with his key employees to try and improve critical deficiencies in the services offered to their customers, only to find out that they were already doing all they could.

Burt knew he simply could not afford to lose this client's business! Frustrated under the weight of these new pressures, his mind preoccupied with ways to best resolve the problem, he decided to ask his friend, John, to meet him for a drink after work. John was in the same line of business and might be able to give Burt some pointers and direction on how to save the Magnisson account. The two men talked of business first, then politics, and the upcoming basketball playoffs, and by the time they got around to the rising cost of living, Burt was on his fourth drink.

Not far from the restaurant, Rachel, a high school senior, glanced at her watch. It was almost closing time at the video store. She would ring up the few customers still lingering in the store, balance out her cash register, restock inventory, and make it home in time to finish her history homework. Rachel could hardly wait for her shift to end so she could get home, not just so she could get her homework out of the way, but also because Trent—her boyfriend of three months—would be calling. Between thoughts of what to wear on her date with Trent on Friday night (*Would her friend Nicole let her borrow her new sweater?*) and what to wear to school tomorrow (*Had her friend Tallia returned her black jeans?*) and considering just how much time her homework would require tonight (*Tomorrow in front of the class she had to explain how a bill passed into legislation— should she wash her hair tonight or in the morning?*), she absently carried out her closing duties with mechanical precision. Rachel punched out on the time clock at just about the same time there was a lull in the conversation between Burt and his friend.

Burt looked down at his watch and saw it was getting late. He had to get home.

Rachel walked to her car in the parking lot. She had no way of knowing that Burt, who had just finished four, maybe five, drinks, was planning to get into his car, as well.

Neither of them had any way of knowing that their routes home crossed.

As Burt turned to walk away from the bar, Rachel started the engine of her car. "Hey," John said, noticing Burt's slight stagger, "will you be okay driving home?" The bartender, who had also been watching with a sharp eye, suggested, "Why don't you let me call you a cab?" Feeling a little embarrassed, at first Burt said, "I'm okay." But then he remembered that the drunk-driving laws were tougher, blood alcohol limits were lower, and besides, he'd heard a lot more over the past few years about just how little it took to impair your driving. "Let me give you a lift home," his friend offered. Burt accepted.

Rachel pulled out of the parking lot—and drove *safely* home.

The increase in public awareness of the dangers of drinking and driving may well have been responsible for her—and for Burt, and untold thousands of others—getting home safely. Rachel and her entire family, like so many families, live active, busy, mobile lives. Rachel's parents both drive to work. While Rachel's eleven-year-old brother and nine-year-old sister walk the four blocks to their elementary school each day, their mother drives them to and from softball practice, dance lessons, and the Boys & Girls Club after school. Rachel's father also spends a lot of time behind the wheel driving to business appointments and picking up the kids from various sports events. On the weekends, the family goes on outings to parks, the zoo, the amusement center, and church. Just about every trip involves driving a car, putting the family on the road among other drivers.

Rachel drives to school each day. On the days when she doesn't have to work after school, she and her friends go to the mall or they go to each other's houses. There are trips to the library, the movies, and the school games. Rachel's parents trust her to drive safely and hope the streets will be safe for their daughter, indeed for all their children, as well as for themselves. The thought that they might receive a phone call informing them any member of their family has been in an accident doesn't even bear imagining. On May 3, 1980, another mother, Candace Lightner, received just such a call.

A young divorcee, Candace had carefully selected a home for her children and herself in a quiet, safe community, one that would allow them to "get on with their lives" after the upheaval of the divorce. She felt confident she had selected well—a quiet enclave with little traffic, assuring that, with love and care, they'd find the security the family needed to regroup. Certainly, she never thought drunk drivers would disturb the tranquility of a "safe haven" such as the one she had chosen. Yet as Candace Lightner's thirteen-year-old daughter, Cari, was walking to a church carnival one day in May, a drunk driver struck her from behind—and then he kept right on driving. The car hit her with such a force, young Cari was thrown 125 feet. She suffered massive internal injuries.

Four days after her daughter's death, Candace Lightner learned that the police had arrested the drunk driver who had killed her daughter. The man had several previous convictions for driving while under the influence of alcohol. Not only that, he had been arrested for D.U.I. just two days before he got behind the wheel drunk once again and careened into her daughter! Already angry that he could still have a license with such a record, when Candace was told the man was likely to do little jail time, she was outraged. This man, flagrantly defying the drunk driving laws instituted for public safety, would be allowed to continue to threaten the lives of others! Her loss, her pain and grief were unfathomable, indescribable, and yet, this man, who had ravaged a mother's life and stolen every new minute of her daughter's life, was going to pay with only a few days of jail time? "Where was justice?" she demanded.

Through her grief, Candace ranted at the corrupt travesty: "How could it be that a child so young with so much of life left to live, her baby, so innocent and deserving of a full, rich life could be denied her adolescence, her adulthood, her old age — while the man who had robbed her of these things with a callous, self-centered disregard for others, paid only a few days for his crimes? How could our laws be so ineffective, so unenforced, as to allow such an injustice?" Candace knew because of these lenient laws, other parents would have to go through the agony she was feeling.

Although never so glaringly aware of this inequity in our legal system, Candace had some prior knowledge of its lack of conviction. This was not the first time her family had suffered at the hands of an intoxicated driver. Her mother's car had been rear-ended when her daughter, Serena (Cari's twin sister), was just eighteen months old. Serena had been bruised in the crash and lacerated by broken glass shards. Then, just six years later, Candace's four-year-old son, Travis, was hit by a car while playing in front of the house. His injuries included a collapsed lung, a broken leg, broken ribs, and a fractured skull. Her son's head injury caused brain damage that left him with a long-term handicap. The driver who struck Travis was under the influence of tranquilizers. And now her daughter Cari had been killed by the same sort of senseless tragedy — one that could have been avoided if it weren't for a lack of enforcement of drunk driving laws.

Fueled with raging indignation, Candace was determined to put an end to such irresponsibility and senseless death.

She became a tireless crusader, channeling her anger into establishing MADD (Mothers Against Drunk Drivers), an organization whose mission is to keep drunk drivers off the road. If MADD could save even one child, her daughter's life and its tragic loss would not have been in vain. Today MADD has three million members, with chapters in forty-seven states. Due to the efforts of MADD, there are tougher laws against drinking and driving, and the legal drinking age has been raised to twenty-one in every state. When MADD was founded in 1980, twenty-five thousand people were killed by drunk drivers. Today, that figure is reduced by nearly one thousand lives each year, and there's a 36 percent decline in drunk driving. Perhaps today it may have even saved the life of one of our own loved ones.

MADD has raised our nation's awareness and dramatically changed the public attitude towards drinking and driving. It is a pearl of awareness, spawning new laws to save lives, and has made the streets safer for families like Rachel's—active, busy, mobile families, much like our own.

Heroically, Candace Lightner rose above her despair, working tirelessly for the safety of others by initiating local, state, and national reform, even though her daughter Cari could no longer benefit from them. How sorry we are for her great loss. And how thankful we are that she courageously chose not to mourn privately and instead cried, "No more!"

That we care for each other, that we protect others from a pain that we've endured, is a testament to the caretaking nature of the human spirit to provide a "safer haven" for us all. May we never forget that we are all safer because of one woman's efforts—a pearl born out of her loss.

The Pianist

"People change and forget to tell each other."
—LILLIAN HELLMAN

A very special guest piano player had been invited to Seaside, a quaint little neighborhood church that nestled beneath the towering eucalyptus overlooking the pale blue Pacific. After taking her two children to their Sunday school classes, Marta slipped into the pew beside her mother, who—because she was so entranced by the music—hardly seemed to notice that her daughter had joined her. Instead, she continued to watch the pianist intently, her face transformed into a look of complete awe and pleasure. Marta's grandmother always said Marta's mother could have been a concert pianist. She had played from the time she was four; everyone agreed that she was gifted.

As Marta watched her mother's face in church that day and saw her eyes actually fill with tears at the beauty of the music, she felt so sad for her, sad that her dreams of becoming an accomplished concert pianist had never been realized. Instead she'd gotten married and raised six children. Seeing her mother sitting there with this soulful look of joy and appreciation for the music being played, and thinking of all she'd sacrificed to raise her family, Marta was filled with a sense of appreciation and gratitude for all the ways her mother had been a devoted parent—rather than devoting herself to the music that gave her so much pleasure.

It also made her sad for her mother's unrequited dreams.

Having lived through the depression and World War II, it seemed to Marta that her mother had known a lot of hardships. She'd suffered loss as well. Marta thought of how her mother fought off tears to this day when the subject of her parents and little brother came up. She had lost all her family before she celebrated her twenty-first birthday.

Marta's heart was filled with tender sorrow for her, and she was thankful it had been her good fortune to have this woman—a devoted mother, selfless when it came to her family—as her Mom.

When they walked out of church, the daughter felt moved to express her gratitude for her mother's sacrifice and said, "Mom, thank you so much for all you've given up for us."

Looking genuinely surprised, her mother asked, "Oh? How's that?"

"Well, I know it was always your dream to be a concert pianist and how much . . ."

"Oh," her mother laughed and explained, "being a concert pianist was never my greatest dream—although it was always your grandmother's dream for me." Then she sighed wistfully and confessed, "Oh, there was a time I held her dream for my own. But once I lost my parents and my brother, I had a different dream. A *greater* dream. It was to marry someone I really loved and to have a large family for me to love, children who would play together and love each other, too. *You are my dream,* but I still love to hear beautiful piano music!"

"But Mom, what about the music you've given up?"

"Throughout the years of reading bedtime stories, kissing bandaged elbows and knees, and finding the inevitable lost shoe, being told 'I love you,' from the six of you has been music *enough*," replied the mother whose dream was realized with a large and loving family and a home filled with love and laughter. "It's the most beautiful music of all. Really!"

Certainly a happy heart, like a pearl, is a dream come true.

The Right Words

"Home is where you come to and they have to let you in."
—ROBERT FROST

Cindy Newell and her seventeen-year-old were cooking dinner, a daily ritual that each looked forward to. It was "their time together," a way to savor the less than seven months before Lindsey—the last of her three children at home and now in her senior year—would go off to college.

Long divorced, for the most part Cindy had raised her three children on her own. Her children were good kids, bright, well-behaved, and she was proud of them. Still, after all the years of raising children, Cindy had genuinely looked forward to sending her last offspring out into the wonderful world to begin a life of her own. Then finally Cindy would have some time to herself for a change.

Her daughter was unusually helpful this evening and quiet, something that Cindy attributed to the on-again, off-again relationship and then the big breakup with the boy she had been dating for well over ten months now.

"Everything okay, honey?" Cindy asked her daughter, thinking she would find these words comforting. She expected her daughter to say, "Yes" or "I guess," or maybe even break into a discourse of the woes of her relationship with Kenny, since Cindy knew that he wasn't all that ready (or willing) to be a full-time boyfriend to her daughter. Instead, her daughter began to cry. Then came the stunning—and stinging—words: "Mom, I'm pregnant."

Just three words. "How could just three words so *suddenly* alter that moment. So *totally* alter her life?

Looking at her lovely seventeen-year-old baby, Cindy's mind raced for the right response. After all, she was a mother of the nineties, she'd read parenting books, knew about healthy communication. Surely somewhere within her were the right words, waiting for her to speak them. Though right now, she'd settle for an appropriate facial expression to deliver what her voice could not. Would not. But unable to think of any words of wisdom or profound guidance, instead Cindy simply found herself looking at her daughter and then numbly making her way across the kitchen to simply hold her.

After several minutes that seemed like hours came the words "What are you going to do?"

"I don't know," Lindsey cried.

Parental diligence to the rescue, Cindy met her daughter's eyes and said what she believed must be the right words to say at such a time. "I'll support you in whatever decision you make."

In silence amid tears they slowly set the table. She tried to breathe calmly. She'd said the right thing—hadn't she?

Dinner that night held an unusual silence.

"Is Chad the father?" Cindy now asked, then cringed at how offhanded her question sounded.

"Yes," Lindsey nodded. "But we're not getting back together. He doesn't want anything to do with me or the baby." Oddly enough, Cindy felt relieved—that was one part of "the mistake" her daughter wouldn't make.

Cindy had gotten pregnant in high school, too; and she'd married her fiancé at the time. She was certain their engagement would never actually have resulted in marriage if she hadn't become pregnant. The engagement, the small diamond ring, the talk of a wedding after she graduated, her plans for having an apartment with her very own furniture—all was more a fantasy, an adolescent girl merrily dreaming of make-believe plans to be with the boy who sat in front of her in math class. He had been her first crush and therefore, of course, her "true love." It was a fun game, one that became a reality for her when her family doctor announced she was pregnant. Then it had all become very real. Too real. That was twenty-five years ago.

There was a twist of the knife in the pain she felt seeing her child follow the same path she had. Especially so young, Cindy knew this event would alter the course of Lindsey's life. Somehow, it just had its own added agony. Perhaps because, though all logic might argue, it was accompanied by a burden of guilt—as if she could have somehow passed along some genetic lack or inadvertent moral conditioning that caused Lindsey to make the same mistake.

Lost in the haze of these feelings and thoughts, Lindsey's next words took a moment to sink in. "Mom, I'm going to have the baby," she said, then clarified, "and keep it."

Cindy wondered how relief and dread could collide in the same exact instant within her.

She sighed and, perhaps with even less conviction than the first time she spoke the words, she repeated, "I'll support you in whatever decision you make." Each syllable she uttered seemed weighted under her crushing disappointment both in knowing what hardships her daughter would now face and in counting the loss of all those dreams of college, career, and a carefree youth. Not to mention a fine man to marry and a good husband and father—all of which she'd harbored for Lindsey. Dreamed for her. Planned for her. She spent what must have seemed like all of her daughter's life instilling in Lindsey that she wanted—and needed—these things, too.

Tossing and turning in her bed that night, Cindy's thoughts turned from how her daughter's pregnancy would impact her daughter's life to how it would impact her own life. She'd been raising children all her life since she was a teenager. Long divorced, for the most part she'd done it on her own. Lindsey was in her senior year, she was supposed to go on to college the following year, move out of the house, get a part-time job—all those things her older brother and sister had done smoothly and right on schedule. And after all the years of raising children, Cindy had genuinely looked forward to having the last of the kids out of the house and a time when she could finally get on with goals and plans of her own.

She was upset about the sudden death of all those plans, even mad—even if she couldn't say it out loud. Lindsey was young, and Cindy could see her daughter's eyes had suddenly become those of a mother's: Burdened. Hopeful. Fearful. Her teenager had paid for unveiling a mystery—the loss of her innocence. It was the price she had paid, and Cindy had hoped that in seven months her bill would have been paid in full. Now she saw it wasn't. Worse, her beloved daughter was about to begin a lifetime on the same "deferred-payment" plan as Cindy had. As a single parent and without the benefit of high school education, Cindy was relegated to low-paying menial work. Raising three children had been an arduous and very long journey. With this daughter getting ready to head out the door, she had hopes for her own regrouping, maybe even going back to school or, at the least, affording to buy herself a few small things she had done without—always. Just as she'd finally seen a light at the end of the child-rearing tunnel, that light had just moved farther away—far enough to seem completely out of sight.

Cindy knew she would have to accept this—would have to reconcile herself to the disappointment—and beyond saying the right words, she'd have to do the right thing. Still, she couldn't seem to shake off her feelings of defeat and despair.

Expectant mother or not, Lindsey was still only seventeen, and her behavior and maturity reflected it. When Cindy told her it was her responsibility to tell her grandparents and her father about the baby, Lindsey balked. She carried on with her life as if she could keep it a secret from them forever. Her father's contact with her was sporadic and volatile. They seemed to argue every time they got together—which wasn't very often. Being in her teens, Lindsey's friends and social life were her focus, so she didn't mind limiting her contact with her father. She was close to Cindy's parents and confessed to Cindy that she didn't want to confront their disappointment. Cindy pointed out everyone would know soon enough—it would be quite apparent. But Lindsey didn't budge.

It was two months before Cindy finally told her sister, who told her other sister, who told their mother (so much for healthy communication). Cindy philosophically accepted the probability that hers, like most families of the nineties, might be said to have some "dysfunction." Her mother felt the need to avoid speaking to Lindsey about it and instead spoke to Cindy—which, of course, was just fine with Lindsey.

"Cindy, I told you that girl was staying out too late," her mother chided. Cindy found it ironic that her mother's words seemed a bit late in coming and also felt hurt that the blame had been shifted to her shoulders—which served to rekindle her own guilt.

Yet her mother was right about one thing—words did mean a lot to Cindy. This was never more apparent than when Lindsey's father also avoided talking to Lindsey and instead told Cindy, "I'm through with that girl. I mean, she's my daughter and I care about her, but if I were to wake up tomorrow and it so happened she'd never been born, it wouldn't bother me at all." Was his disdain about her pregnancy? If so, how could a father be so removed from the fatherly support—and wisdom—his daughter could use from him now? His reaction was more harsh than Cindy had imagined, his words ripping into her heart. How could he say or think such a thing about his own daughter—his own blood? Then she felt a new wave of guilt: How could she have chosen such a man to father her children?

Cindy sheltered Lindsey from the knowledge that such words were ever spoken, and in a way, his words meant that she must support her daughter in her decision, just as she had said she would—determined to do "the right thing." Even so, Cindy couldn't escape her overwhelming sense of disappointment. She'd wanted so much more, so much *easier* for her daughter, her youngest, her baby—a pregnant *teenager*. If her actions were rote, a lifeless response to her determination, she did all she could to hide it from Lindsey.

Though she didn't verbalize these feelings to Lindsey, she could not escape her inner turmoil. "Okay," she asserted, while driving to work the next morning. "So *exactly* when does the sentence of oppression in my life get lifted? I've tried to live decently and be a good model to the kids. I really have. And now this. I'm so tired of being on an around-the-clock, never-ending schedule! And now I'm supposed to get up for yet another round of being tied down and unending responsibility. Really! When do *I* get a break?" The questions to herself on the way home were a rehash of the same. This went on each day for nearly two weeks.

They were the same questions she uttered in her head as she arrived at the doctor's office for Lindsey's first sonogram. But things were about to change.

The nurse attached Lindsey to a monitor and Cindy heard the baby's heart beat for the first time. Then the nurse put a gel on Lindsey's stomach and circled its surface with a wand that sent waves to pick up the image of the fetus. Cindy watched the screen of the machine with a growing sense of wonder as the form of the baby actually came into focus before her eyes. The head, the arms, the legs, the little bottom.

Cindy was going to have a grandson.

As she stood there staring at the screen, she thought of Lindsey's father's words, " . . . if I were to wake up tomorrow and it so happened she'd never been born, it wouldn't bother me at all . . . ." She remembered her indignation that he could think such a thing. Yet, hadn't she had similar feelings about her own blood—her new grandson?

"I'm going to name him Alex!" the teen announced with the same exuberance as when she had first laid eyes on her first prom dress. And suddenly Cindy looked at the little boy on the screen, Alex—her grandbaby—in an entirely different light. In that moment, little Alex was growing in her heart, a little soul, a little boy who deserved her loving welcome into the world.

Other transformations were as immediate. Suddenly, love was everywhere again. Birds sang songs of hope; flowers, ones she could literally smell from a distance, were in bloom everywhere. Even strangers were friendly. The inanimate acceptance she had been mimicking surged to life, budding into a complete acceptance for this tiny soul.

She couldn't have imagined how her newfound love for the little unborn being would grow so steadily over the next weeks. With a renewed vigor—and a new sense of purpose for her own being—Cindy helped pick out the baby's things and prepared for her grandson's arrival. As she launched into full-scale preparations, she discovered that her *acceptance* for little Alex had turned into loving him.

But it was only the beginning. As the young, black-haired, barely forty-year-old grandma stood holding her teenager's hand and watching little Alex come tumbling into the world, love gave way to a sense of joy she hadn't *ever* remembered feeling.

She thought this emotion was at the top of the list of the heart's ability to produce perfection—and then, moments after his arrival, Grandma was handed a little, pink newborn with ten tiny toes and ten tiny fingers, his little eyes pinched shut and whimpering for protection. As Grandma held his swaddled perfect little body in her arms for the first time—studying the squalling little bundle with rapture—she knew that her heart had only begun to open for the ways she was about to experience love.

Love is a powerful converter of emotions—one that makes many things possible. Certainly it permitted Cindy to take pride in her daughter as she witnessed the transformation in her—from self-centered adolescent to selfless, loving mother, from impatient youth to tirelessly patient parent. Certainly it allowed Lindsey to feel a sense of responsibility to her son and to nurture family bonds, beginning with her father. But it allowed Cindy to look within herself as well.

As Cindy watched Alex learn to crawl, to pull himself up, to stand—and then take his first few steps—she decided this little boy had come into her life precisely so that she might have more joy and fullness. It was a daily dose: as he bobbed happily keeping the beat to music and threw himself into his first dance of life—the "baby bop"—with blissful vigor; as he toddled around the house behind her, interested in everything she did and everywhere she went; as he greeted his first bouncing ball with his own completely unanticipated joy, making sounds of fascinated delight akin to a caveman discovering fire, so that Cindy and Lindsey dubbed him "primal baby."

While Alex celebrates his first birthday, Cindy glows with price as Lindsey shows her little boy how to blow out the candles on his cake. Alex whistles into them. Grandpa stands nearby, laughing and dabbing at the tears of love and joy his grandson brings.

Even disappointment, it seems, is fodder for the soul, a bittersweet food that can be transformed into acceptance and then the pearl of learning *rightly* how to love. Certainly it was among the cherished lessons ushered in by baby Alex. It's a common lesson: The right words to say are always present in the language of love— a joyful language made possible by the human heart and the soul that guides it. A little boy by the name of Alex not only changed the lives of a family ready to go off "into the world," but reunited their acceptance and love for one another.

About the Author

Bettie B. Youngs, Ph.D., Ed.D., is the Pulitzer Prize nominated author of seventeen books published in twenty-nine languages and respected voice in the field of human potential and personal effectiveness. Dr. Youngs is a former Teacher of the Year and university professor. She serves on the Board of Directors to several universities and a number of organizations and is a frequent guest expert on television and radio talk shows. *NBC Nightly News, CNN, Oprah, Geraldo, Good Morning America, Barbara Walters, U.S. News & World Report, USA Today, The Washington Post, Time Magazine, Family Circle, Redbook, McCalls, Working Woman, Parents Magazine, Better Homes & Gardens,* and *Woman's Day* have all recognized her work.

Though her earlier work focused predominately in the areas of education and developmental psychology for youth, family, and educators, in recent years she is best known for her series of lovingly and beautifully told short stories, works that clearly, familiarly, and warmly elucidate the human spirit in its finest hour and have captivated the American psyche, winning her wide-range appeal with readers young and old alike.

Values From the Heartland, a 1997 World Storytelling award winner, explores the deeper side of integrity, honor, and character and how these are instilled by key people in our lives. The Pulitzer-nominated *Gifts of the Heart* bears witness to the ideal that a loving action modeled is still the best form of teaching and the basis for lasting change.

Taste Berry Tales reminds us that it is our obligation—as much as it is our honor—to help others on a daily basis to see their lives in the most positive light and that by helping others to sweeten life's joys and ease the bitterness of its losses, to see our world as full of hope, less impossible, and more glorious, we nourish our own spirit.

Her most recent *Taste Berries for Teens: Inspirational Short Stories and Encouragement on Life, Love, Friendship, and Tough Issues,* coauthored with daughter Jennifer, is a runaway bestseller for teens. It offers teens the opportunity to glimpse their own contribution to making a difference in the world.

Bettie has received an outpouring of praise from both critics and readers for her works:

"The value of human caring is evident in so many of these stories and I find that refreshing and uplifting."—William J. Perry, former Secretary of Defense

"What a marvelous book!"—Ronald Glosser, Vice Chairman of the Board, *Guidepost*

"Your words soothe suffering and create happiness."—Mother Teresa

"Bettie's books open our hearts to the beauty, depth, power, and resilience of the human spirit. No one can read her work without being moved."—Mrs. Norman Vincent Peale

"As compiler of the 'Chicken Soup' books, I read thousands of stories every year. Bettie's are always the best. They touch me more deeply than anything else I've ever read. Her works remind us of the nobility of our human beingness. Truly awesome"—Jack Canfield

But perhaps kudos for her work are best summed up by Joan Marx, Peabody and Writers Guild award-winning producer of film and television screen-writing: *"Bettie has an absolutely beautiful style of writing—passionate, poetic, strong, and intelligent. But what elevates her to an elite league of writers is that through her writing she has an indelible voice. You don't see that all that often. It's rare, it's special, and it's simply a captivating style for the reader. You are there with her in every sentence."*

Also available from Adams Media Corporation

Heartwarmers
by Azriela Jaffe

Heartwarmers is a celebration of life's most precious and meaningful moments. Written by ordinary people, these extraordinary real-life tales explore the magic that graces our daily lives. For the first time in print, *Heartwarmers* brings together over 70 of the very best stories from the popular *Heartwarmers4u.com website.*

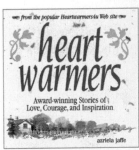

Trade paperback, $9.95,
ISBN: 1-58062-308-5,
240 pages

Available Wherever Books Are Sold

If you cannot find this title at your favorite retail outlet, you may order it directly from the publisher. BY PHONE: Call 1-800-872-5627. We accept Visa, MasterCard, and American Express. $4.95 will be added to your total order for shipping and handling. BY MAIL: Write out the full title of the book you d like to order and send payment, including $4.95 for shipping and handling, to: Adams Media Corporation, 260 Center Street, Holbrook, MA 02343, or visit our Web site at: www.adamsmedia.com, 30-day money-back guarantee.

Also available from Adams Media Corporation

The Small Miracles Series

The *Small Miracles* Series is a collection of true stories of remarkable coincidences that have changed the lives of ordinary people. The stories, both heartwarming and awe-inspiring, convey that coincidences are more than just random happenings—in fact, they are nothing less than divine messages.

Trade paperback, $8.95,
ISBN: 1-55850-646-2

Trade paperback, $8.95
ISBN: 1-58062-047-7

Trade paperback, $8.95,
ISBN: 1-58062-180-5

Available Wherever Books Are Sold

If you cannot find this title at your favorite retail outlet, you may order it directly from the publisher. BY PHONE: Call 1-800-872-5627. We accept Visa, MasterCard, and American Express. $4.95 will be added to your total order for shipping and handling. BY MAIL: Write out the full title of the book you d like to order and send payment, including $4.95 for shipping and handling, to: Adams Media Corporation, 260 Center Street, Holbrook, MA 02343, or visit our Web site at: www.adamsmedia.com, 30-day money-back guarantee.